English Premier League
Academy
Training Sessions

Volume Two

by
Rob Gale

Published by
WORLD CLASS COACHING

First published January, 2005 by

WORLD CLASS COACHING 15004 Buena Vista Drive, Leawood, KS 66224 (913) 402-0030

ISBN 0-9746723-4-3

Copyright © WORLD CLASS COACHING 2005

Author - Rob Gale
Edited by Mike Saif

Front Cover - Designed by Babcock Illustration & Design. Photographs provided by Kidz-N-Sports Photography

Published by
WORLD CLASS COACHING

<u>*Acknowledgements*</u>

Express thanks to John Peacock, Mick Gale and to all the Score UK coaching staff, both past and present. Thanks to Steve and Karen for getting me started in football with two great role models and to Erin and Hadyn for making it all worthwhile.

Good luck with your coaching!

Rob Gale

English Premier League
Academy
Training Sessions

Volume Two

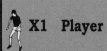 X1   Player

Path of Player

Path of Ball

 Path of Dribble

 Target Area

GLOSSARY OF TERMS

ACTIVE DEFENDING – NORMAL TACKLING DEFENDING

CONDITION – PLACE A RESTRICTION ON

CONTROLLING SURFACE – PART OF BODY USED TO CONTROL BALL

DROP KICK – HALF VOLLEY FROM THE HANDS USED BY GOALIES

DUMMY – FAKE OR MOVE

FLANK – WING OR WIDE AREA OF FIELD

FOOTBALL = SOCCER

GIVE AND GO'S – ONE TWO – OR EXCHANGE OF PASSES

PASSIVE DEFENDING – CAN NOT TACKLE OPPONENT

SCRIMMAGE – MATCH OR GAME

TACKLE – CHALLENGE FOR THE BALL

THE READY POSITION – GOALKEEPERS STARTING POSITION – HANDS BY SIDE

VOLLEY – TO STRIKE THE BALL WHILST IT IS IN THE AIR

Chapter One

Technical Sessions

Technical Coaching Sessions

Dribbling Session

Organization 1 v 1
Attacker (X) starts dribbling towards the goal from 40 yards out. Once attacker has taken first touch, defender (O) moves into play and closes down attackers run. Attacker decides whether to take on defender or shoot at goal. Repeat with defender (O) from opposite side.

Progression(s)
• Allow both defenders to work at same time

Key Factors
• Attack with speed but with control
• Keep ball moving and take shot early

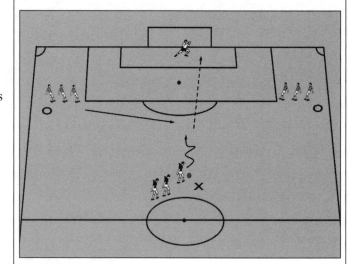

Dribbling Session

Organization
Similar set up as before, now with X1 passing ball into forward X2. X2 controls and dribbles ball towards goal. Defender O now moves once X2 has taken first touch. X2 dribbles to goal and shoots to score. Repeat both sides.

Progression(s)
• X1 can pressure X2 from behind once X2 has controlled

Key Factors
• Observe space and defender
• Receive side on
• Control ball forward - towards desired target
• Decision - dribble or shoot
• Quality of finish

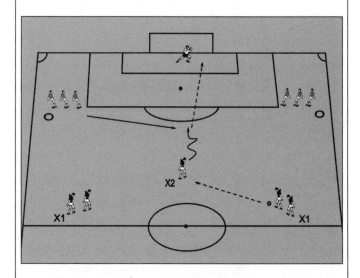

Technical Coaching Sessions

Diagram	Organization

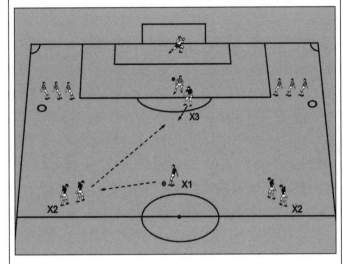

Dribbling Session

Organization
X1 passes to X2. X2 plays into X3. X3 must start being tight to defender O. X3 comes off O stays in the D. On X3's first touch O can defend. Repeat both ways.

Progression(s)
- X1 follows pass and becomes second defender - X2 follows pass and becomes second attacker

Key Factors
- Drift off O - side on position
- Control ball forward
- Make decision early - dribble or shoot
- Quality of finish

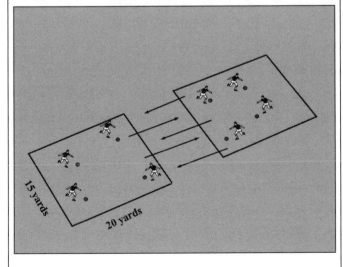

Dribbling Session

Organization
Two groups of players each with a ball are put into two 15 by 20 yard grids. On coaches command players have to dribble with speed to opposite grid.

Progression(s)
- Players have to perform certain moves/fakes in the middle between grids - Matthews, Maradonna, Scissors etc.

Key Factors
- Get the ball out in front
- Use the outside of the foot when running with the ball

Technical Coaching Sessions

Dribbling Session

Organization
Four teams line up in each corner of a 30 by 30 yard grid, with a supply of balls in the middle. Each team have one player at a time get a ball from the center and dribble it back to their home base. Players then one at a time can take a ball from other teams base.

Progression(s)
• Play for a desired time period or till one team has all the balls

Key Factors
• Players must turn with the ball and explode
• Dribble with outside of the foot in the open space

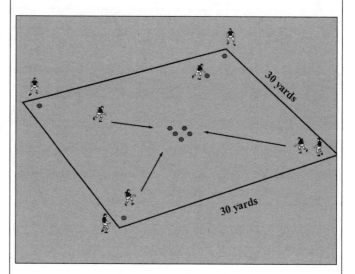

Dribbling Session

Organization
Two teams of equal numbers play in a 30 by 40 yard grid. Players have to dribble ball across end line to score a point.

Progression(s)
• Play "make it and take it" - if you score at one end you keep possession and attack opposite end immediately
• Increase numbers on each team to finish with an 11 v 11 full field game

Key Factors
• Look for spaces behind defender to dribble into
• Keep ball close then explode away
• Attack the open space with speed
• Players must attack opponents at every opportunity

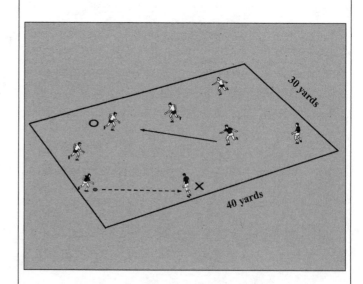

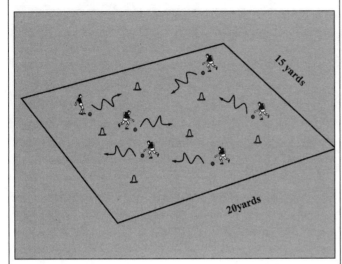

Dribbling Session

Organization - Close control
Each player has a ball and dribbles around randomly placed cones within a 20 by 15 yard grid. On coaches command, players have to dribble at different speeds.

Progression(s)
- Players have to perform certain tasks on coaches command - toe taps, foundations, step-overs etc

Key Factors
- Keep control of the ball
- Use all surfaces of the foot - manipulate the ball
- Use both feet

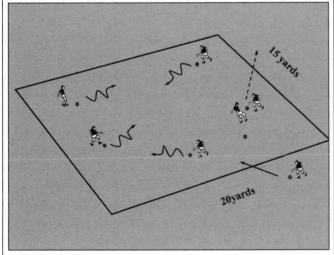

Dribbling Session

Organization - Knock out
Same set up as previous. Players dribble ball around grid but now have to knock out everyone else's ball while keeping control of their own.

Progression(s)
- Once knocked out players remain out to see who wins
- Players can re-enter grid once they have performed set task

Key Factors
- Keep a low center of gravity - "knees bent"
- Keep body between ball and defenders
- Keep the ball moving and change direction often

Diagram	Organization

Dribbling Session

Organization
Same set up as previous "Knock out" drill but now with defenders. Attackers with a ball dribble around and defenders try to clear balls out. Defenders work for one minute or until all balls are knocked out.

Progression(s)
• Once players get knocked out they must do 25 toe taps before re-entering
• Attackers can team up to keep ball away from defenders

Key Factors
• Keep head up
• Find space
• Change of pace
• Change of direction

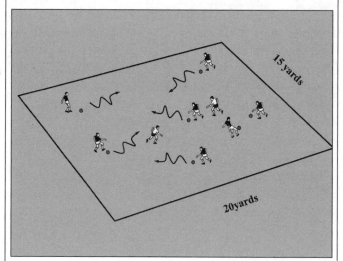

Dribbling Session

Organization
Two teams of equal numbers play on an appropriately sized field. Team X are up by two goals and must keep possession without getting scored on.

Progression(s)
• Team X are now behind by a goal and have to score with 5 minutes to go

Key Factors
• Movement - with and without the ball
• Find space
• Time waste - dribble into corners
• Slow the game down

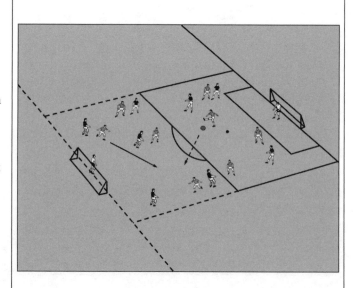

Technical Coaching Sessions

Diagram	Organization

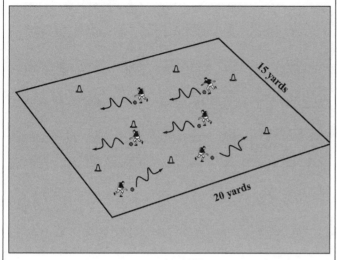

Dribbling Session

Organization
Each player with a ball dribbles around a 20 by 15 yard grid. Players have to attack cones and execute a set skill/move around the cone.

Progression(s)
- Step Over - player steps over the ball to unbalance the defender
- Self pass - player plays ball around opponent to run onto
- Lunge - player steps and leans to one side
- Matthews - two touches with the inside of the foot, then one big touch with the outside of the same foot

Key Factors
- Heads up
- Attack cone at speed

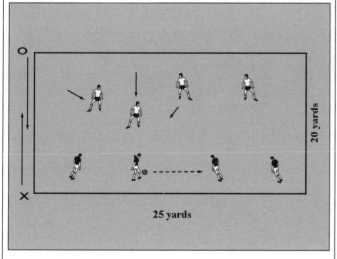

Dribbling Session

Organization
Within a 20 by 25 yard grid play 4 v 4 and score by dribbling ball over opposing teams end line.

Progression(s)
- Players get a point for beating a player with a move

Key Factors
- Keep ball under control
- Look to disguise move
- Change of pace
- Explode
- Players must eliminate opponent
- Attack with purpose

Organization	Diagram

Dribbling Session

Organization
Two teams of six play within a 30 by 35 yard grid with four corner goals. Each team has two goals in which to score in.

Progression(s)
• Change goals to keep players off balance
• Add neutral players to overload attackers or defenders

Key Factors
• Promote risk taking in the final third
• Movement with and without the ball - taking defenders out of their position

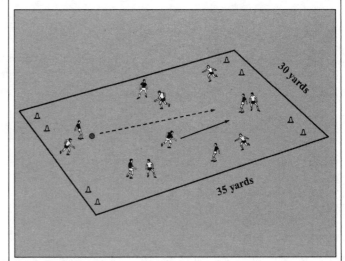

Dribbling Session

Organization
Full field game of 11 v 11 recapping all the skills learned in the previous sessions. Regular rules apply.

Progression(s)
• Restrict players to certain touch limit
• Restrict defenders to certain positions

Key Factors
• Safety should now be a major thought of the players - be aware of the opponents strengths and weaknesses and exploit them

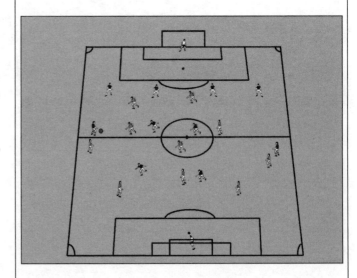

Diagram	Organization

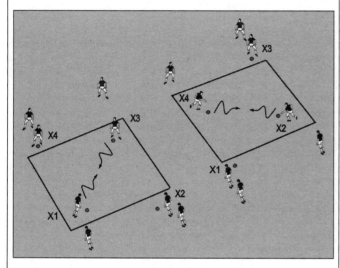

Dribbling Session

Organization
Four teams line up in corners of a 20 by 20 yard square. Players X1 and X3 start to dribble towards each other and perform desired move in the middle. The continue their runs and join the back of opposite line. X2 and X4 start once X1 and X3 have finished.

Progression(s)
• Have all four starters go at once

Key Factors
• Play with your head up
• Timing is important - don't get too close to partner
• Step-overs, Matthews, Maradonna's etc

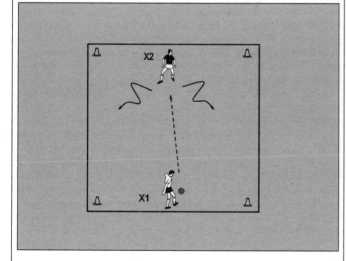

Dribbling Session

Organization 1 v 1
X1 passes to X2. Upon X2's first touch, X1 closes down. X2 has to dribble and stop ball at opposite end.

Progression(s)
• Allow X1 to attack if they tackle and win the ball
• Add a second attacker to give 2 v 1 passing option
• Add a second defender to give covering option

Key Factors
• Attack with speed and purpose
• Head up and look to exploit weakness

Organization	Diagram

Receiving Session

Organization
Players split into groups of threes. S1 and S2 on outside with O in the middle. S1 plays ball into O. O turns and plays into S2. S2 repeats in opposite direction.

Progression(s)
- Rotate all positions
- S2 is a moving target

Key Factors
- Options for O to take:
  - onto back foot
  - take inside
  - set up / spin
- Position to receive
- Create individual space
- Quality of pass

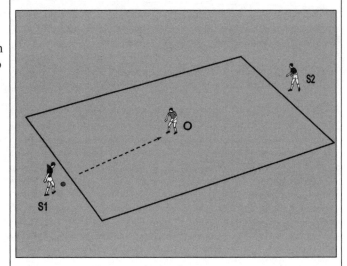

Receiving Session

Organization
Same set up as previous but now S2 is replaced by defender X. S1 plays ball into O who can turn. X can either stay or close O down.

Progression(s)
- Rotate all positions

Key Factors
- O must glance over shoulder before receiving ball
- Open body position
- Decide how/when to control ball based on defenders position

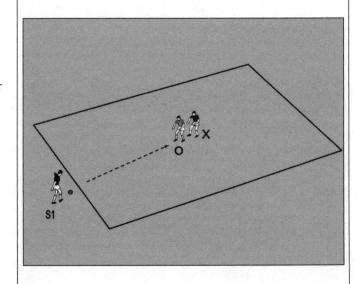

Diagram	Organization

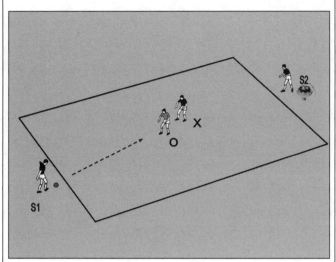

Receiving Session

Organization
Same set up as previous, but now S2 comes back into to play and defender X plays tighter to O. S1 plays ball into O. X defends passively at first. Objective if for O to get ball to S2 if possible.

Progression(s)
- Defender progresses to become more active
- Rotate all positions

Key Factors
- O must drift off X to create space
- Side on position
- O can return pass to S1 if required and start drill again

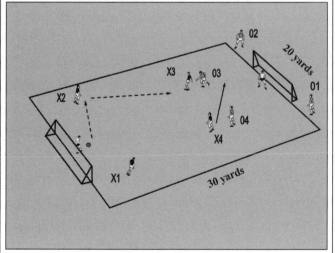

Receiving Session

Organization
GK plays ball into X1 or X2 who then play into X3 or X4. X3 and X4 play 2 v 2 against defenders O3 and O4 but can use X1, X2 or GK if required.

Progression(s)
- Defenders start passive and progress to active defending
- Attack from both sides with O1 and O2 playing against X1 and X2
- Rotate players

Key Factors
- Quality of combination play
- Work on passing angles and quality of pass forward
- Work on support positions of X1 and X2

Technical Coaching Sessions

Organization	Diagram

Receiving Session

Organization
Field is divided into thirds with two defenders and an attacker in each offensive third. No-one in the middle area to begin. GK plays ball into O's who combine to get ball into middle area past attacker X. When into middle area, a defending X comes out creating a 1 v 1. O can combine with supporting attacking player or beat defender X and shoot and score.

Progression(s)
- If defending team tackles, counter attack quickly
- Rotate all positions
- Attack from both sides

Key Factors
- Attack space quickly
- Decision and skill in 1 v 1
- Support position of front player
- Quality and timing of movement

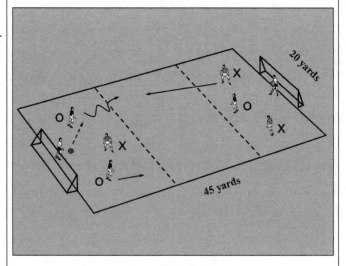

Receiving Session

Organization
Similar set up as previous but now with two attackers and two defenders in each end and a neutral player in middle third. Use GK as outfield player when attacking creating a 3 v 2 at back. The ball must go into neutral player who plays one or two touch only. The ball must be set back before it goes forward into attacking third. Neutral player now supports the front two attacking players

Progression(s)
- Once ball has been played into forwards have a defender move into middle third as an extra option to keep the ball
- Progress by taking neutral player out making it a 4 v 4 plus GK's.

Key Factors
- Ability to receive
- Look for combination play - give and go's
- Movement between front and midfield players
- Communication and support
- Quick transition from defense to offense

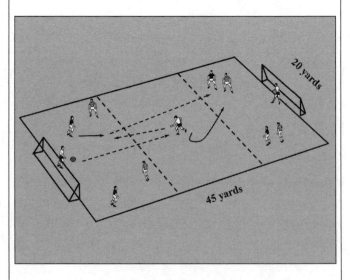

Diagram	Organization

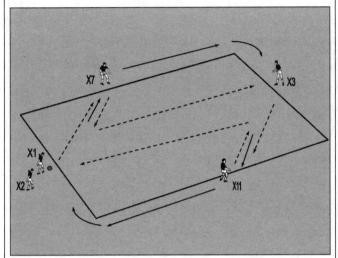

Receiving Session

Organization
X1 plays ball into X7. X7 receives and sets back to X1 then runs down the line. X1 plays ball to X3. X3 plays to X11. X11 receives and sets back to X3 then runs down the line. X3 plays to X2 and play continues.

Progression(s)
- Players rotate all positions
- Play two touch - then one touch

Key Factors
- Players receive side on
- Players vary run after setting ball
    - Run inside
    - Arc run inside/outside

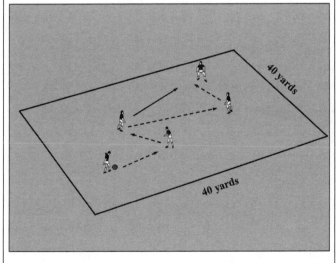

Receiving Session

Organization
Within a 40 by 40 yard grid, players jogging around. A ball is introduced and players pass to each other randomly in sequence two short passes followed by one longer pass on the floor.

Progression(s)
- Play one or two touch only
- Allow longer pass to be lofted
- Change sequence

Key Factors
- Players must receive side on
- Passes must be no more than ten yards for short passes
- Passes must be no less than 20 yards for long passes
- Support player with ball and make runs according to next pass in sequence

Organization	Diagram

Passing & Receiving Session

Organization - Pass and Move
Groups of three work in a 10 by 10 yard grid. Players pass to each other and run to spare corner. For example, X1 passes to X3 at the spare corner. X3 then passes to the spare corner he just vacated for X2.

Progression(s)
• Players play two touch then one touch

Key Factors
• See the ball at all times
• Correct body shape
• Speed and timing of run
• Angle of run

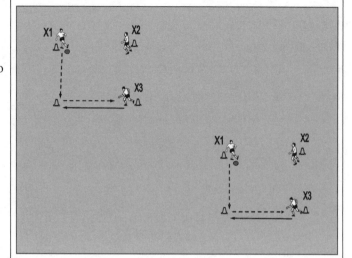

Passing & Receiving Session

Organization - The Number Game
Within a 20 by 20 yard grid players are numbered 1, 2, 3 etc. Players pass in order and move after pass.

Progression(s)
• Players must run around a corner before getting back into position to receive pass
• Change the order - 1-3-5-7-2-4-6-8 etc
• Have two balls working - one and four start with them

Key Factors
• Open body shape to see the ball
• Let ball run across body and use outside foot to control
• Good soft first touch
• Play with head up
• Use good communication - "pass here", "one touch", etc.

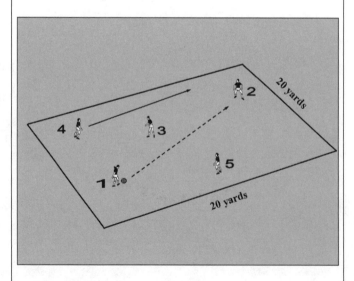

Diagram	Organization

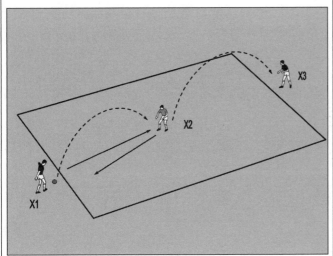

Passing & Receiving Session

Organization - The Middle man
Three 10 by 10 yard grids with groups of three players and one ball. Players 1 and 3 at either end of the grid and player 2 to use the middle 10 by 10 yard grid to receive and pass. Player 1 passes to player 2 who receives and passes to player 3. Player 1 trades with player 2, then player 3 trades with player 1 and repeat after 10 passes each.

Progression(s)
- Vary height and weight of passes into middle player
- Outside players have one touch only
- Add a defender to mark against middle player

Key Factors
- Timing of run
- Angle of run
- First touch
- Quality of pass from servers (weight and accuracy)

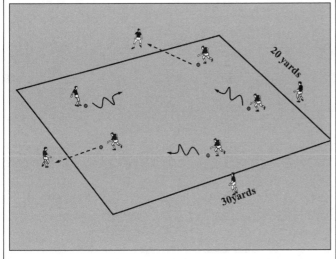

Passing & Receiving Session

Organization
Players divide into two groups of even numbers, half on inside and half on outside of a 30 by 20 yard grid. Players on inside have a ball each and dribble around within the grid, passing to outside players and receiving pass back. After a predetermined time period trade positions.

Progression(s)
- Outside players limited to one touch
- Players in middle to perform fakes/moves before passing
- Make angle for return pass - straight pass move for angled return, angled pass move for straight return
- Switch with outside players

Key Factors
- Head up
- Good quality passing with correct technique
- Outside players on toes and alert
- Quick movement after pass to take up new position

Technical Coaching Sessions

Organization	Diagram

Passing & Receiving Session

Organization
Group of 12 divided into three groups of four. Two players of the four on the inside of a 30 by 20 yard grid and the other two placed outside. The two inside the square work as a pair. People on the outside returning passes. One partner passes to any outside player and partner takes up supporting position, receives return pass from outside.

Progression(s)
• Play two teams against one
• Play with only same team

Key Factors
• Identify position of partner - don't just follow around area
• Good communication allowing player on outside to identify position of both the pair in order to play return pass to correct player at correct time

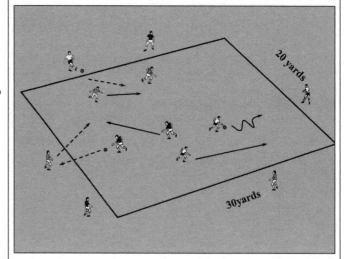

Passing & Receiving Session

Organization - 4 v 4 With Target Players
Within a 30 by 20 yard grid, play 4 v 4 with target players on each side of grid.

Progression(s)
• Points scored for each successful pass and return to target players
• Trade position with target player once you have passed them the ball

Key Factors
• Don't be predictable in your play
• Movement of players - don't stand still
• Keep the ball moving at speed

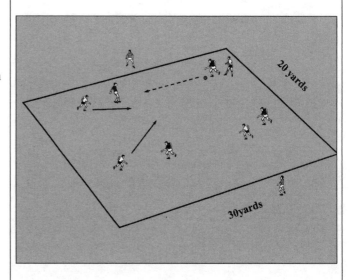

Technical Coaching Sessions

Diagram	Organization

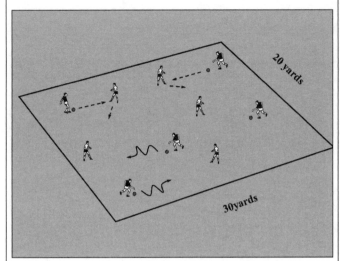

Passing & Receiving Session

Organization - The Wall Pass
Two groups of players (X's and O's) set up within a 30 by 20 yard grid. O's each have a ball and dribble around grid while passing to stationary X's. X's play one touch and return pass to O who has continued run.

Progression(s)
- Players rotate positions

Key Factors
- Weight of pass
- Direction of runs
- Eye contact
- Communication
- Movement of the ball

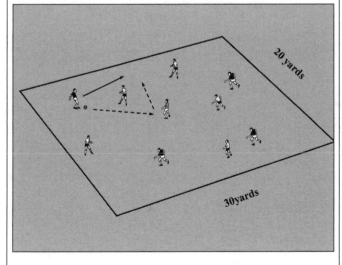

Passing & Receiving Session

Organization - 4 v 4 +1
X's and O's now compete against each other in a game of keep away with a neutral player N playing for team in possession. A goal is scored each time a ball is played through neutral player.

Progression(s)
- Add a second neutral player
- Take neutral player out and play 4 v 4

Key Factors
- look to beat a player
- Try not to become predictable
- Maintain possession
- Shield the ball from opponent
- Draw opposition into play

Technical Coaching Sessions

Organization	Diagram

Passing & Receiving Session

Organization - 7 v 7 +2

Two teams of seven plus two neutral players and a goalkeeper play in a 50 by 30 yard area, The game starts with the goalkeeper kicking a ball out. The first team to achieve a wall pass can attack large goal defended by GK.

Progression(s)

• Have to use neutral player for wall pass
• Take neutral players out and play 7 v 7
• Add small targets for defending team to counter attack to

Key Factors

• Speed of play
• Change of pace
• Change the point of attack
• Players receiving must be aware that they may have to hold onto the ball

Passing & Receiving Session

Organization - The Double Pass

X1 has a ball and passes to X2. X2 passes back to X1. X1 returns pass for the second time and spins out. X2 makes the final pass and plays ball into X1's path as they spin out.

Progression(s)

• Rotate so both players start with ball
• Spin out in both directions

Key Factors

• Crisp one touch passing
• Open body position
• Good weighting of passes

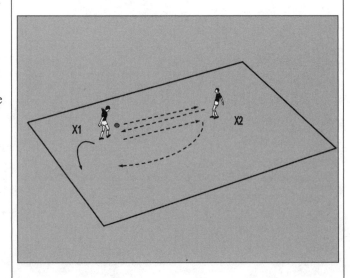

Diagram	Organization

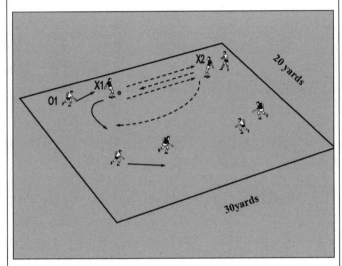

Passing & Receiving Session

Organization - 4 v 4
Two teams of four play keep away and are encouraged to draw opponents into space. A goal is scored for every double pass execution.

Progression(s)
• Limit touches to three touches, two touches and then one touch

Key Factors
• Shield ball
• Correct weight of pass
• Eliminate opponent
• Spin quickly into space away from defender

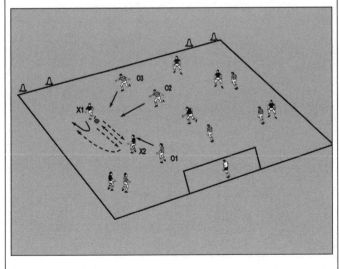

Passing & Receiving Session

Organization - 7 v 7 + GK
Two teams of seven with one goalkeeper defending one large goal. Two small goal/targets at opposite end of large goal. The field dimensions will vary depending on the ability and age of players involved. One team is attacking the large goal and the other is attacking the two small goals.

Progression(s)
• Have team trade playing direction so they each attack against the GK

Key Factors
• Encourage being comfortable in possession
• Do not be predictable
• Quick passes and draw defenders in

Technical Coaching Sessions

Organization	Diagram

Passing & Receiving Session

Organization - The Take Over

Groups of two, one player (X) with a ball dribbles around a 30 by 20 yard grid while partner (O) just jogs. On coaches command O runs towards X and takes ball from them and continues dribbling the ball until coach signals again.

Progression(s)
• Continue with both players taking over from each other for specific time period or until desired number of "take-overs" have been achieved

Key Factors
• Correct pace of run to keep control
• Timing
• Eye contact/communication
• Front foot exchange

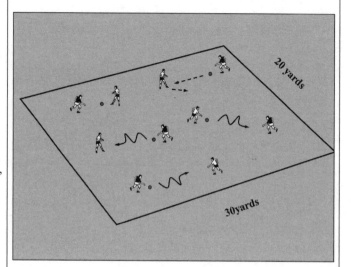

Passing & Receiving Session

Organization

Within a grid 30 by 20 yards, play 4 v 4 with target players at each end. Play regular scrimmage with a point awarded for every "take-over" with target player.

Progression(s)
• Have players take over with each other
• Attack using either target player
• Reduce/increase touch limit

Key Factors
• Be creative
• Take opponents on and look for openings
• Change the point of attack - realizing the opportunities and benefits of the takeover move

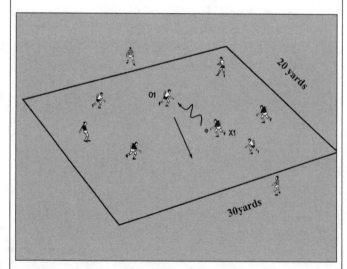

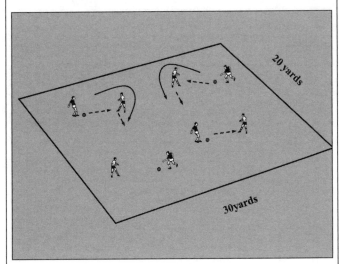

Passing & Receiving Session

Organization - The Over Lap
Groups of two, one player (X) with a ball dribbles around a 30 by 20 yard grid while partner (O) is stationary. On coaches command X plays into O who receives and hold the ball up. X runs around O and receives ball back

Progression(s)
• Rotate positions
• Players can interchange with other partners
• Players can call either "take-over" or "over lap" and play accordingly

Key Factors
• Weight of pass
• Direction of run
• Eye contact
• Communication
• Over lap can be either side of player with ball

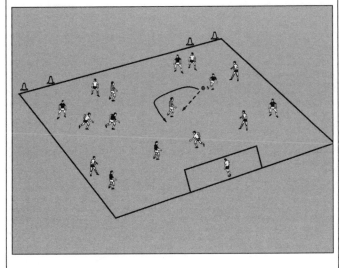

Passing & Receiving Session

Organization
Within a 50 by 30 yard game field with two teams of seven and two neutral players and a goalkeeper. The goalkeeper defends a large regular goal and there are two small goals at opposite end. The neutral players play for team in possession. Game starts with goalkeeper playing ball out. First team to achieve an over lap attacks the large goal.

Progression(s)
• Remove neutral players

Key Factors
• Speed of play
• Change of pace once ball has been played back from receiver or the overlap has been achieved
• Look to beat a player
• Eliminate an opponent
• Players receiving must shield ball and retain possession
• Wait for correct movement, then play in the overlapping player

Organization	Diagram

Defending Session

Organization - 1 v 1
O plays the ball into X then must defend the end line upon X's first touch.

Progression(s)
• No tackling - work on body shape only - "Jockeying"
• Allow tackling

Key Factors
• Quickly close down the attacker
• Slightly bent approach
• Force the attacker to one side
• Knees bent - low center of gravity
• Fake a challenge to force the attacker to try and beat you
• Wait for correct movement to challenge - be patient

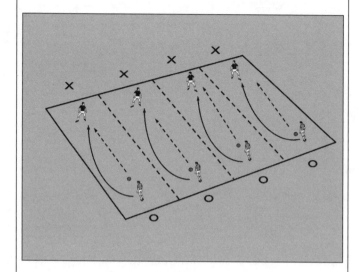

Defending Session

Organization
4 v 4 with gates for goals. Two teams play within a 25 by 30 yard grid. Goals scored by successfully passing to a team mate through gates.

Progression(s)
• Defending to be passive then more active as game progresses
• Man marking
• Zone defending

Key Factors
• Close down player with ball as quickly as possible
• Force player into a direction that gives you the advantage
• Correct pressure
• Correct type of tackle - toe-poke, block or slide tackle
• Timing of tackle

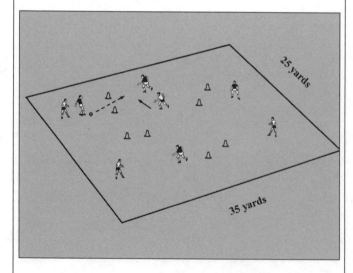

Diagram	Organization

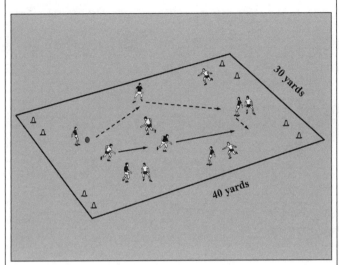

Defending Session

Organization - 6 v 6 with Corner Goals
Two teams of six play with goals in corners of a 40 by 30 yard grid. X's attack to one end and O's attack to the other.

Progression(s)
- Score in any goal
- Add neutral player to defending team to give advantage

Key Factors
- Correct stance - defender should come in side on leaning forward with the intension of looking to tackle
- Players should be low while keeping balance
- First defender must take responsibility in their role
- Second and third defenders need to communicate
- Provide cover/support/balance accordingly

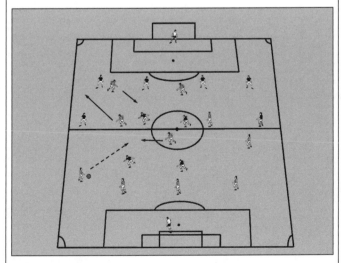

Defending Session

Organization
Full field 11 v 11 scrimmage with focus on individual and team defending.

Progression(s)
- Reduce/increase touch limit
- Man to man marking or zone defending

Key Factors
- Do not over commit to the tackle
- Keep shape
- Coach fair play at all times but remember, defending is a mentality

Technical Coaching Sessions

Organization	Diagram

Defending Session

Organization - The Second Defender
In groups of three, have one player be the attacker O with a ball and two defenders X1 and X2. X1 pressures O and X2 takes up covering position behind X1. O dribbles around while X's take up new positions accordingly.

Progression(s)
• Rotate all positions

Key Factors
• Correct distance between X1 and X2. - close enough to cover first defender but not too close to be beaten by the attacker
• Communication by second defender

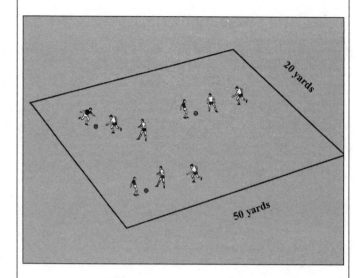

Defending Session

Organization
Two teams play 7 v 7 within a 50 by 30 yard field. Team X has a goalkeeper defending a large goal and they attack two small goals opposite. Team O defend the small goals and attack the large goal. X team plays two touch. Each game starts from the goalkeeper.

Progression(s)
• Both teams play two touch
• Both teams play unlimited touches

Key Factors
• Correct side of support
• Aware of players off the ball
• Do not over commit
• Stay aware of attackers movement
• Keep good team formation
• Allow first defender to challenge the ball and be prepared to close in on ball if the tackle has not been won
• Be in position to see the opponent and the ball at all times
• Create a 2 v 1 as soon as possible

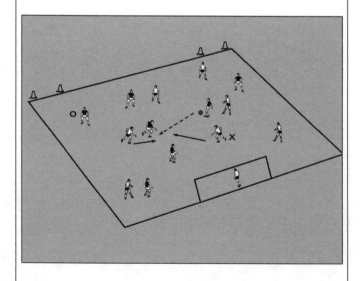

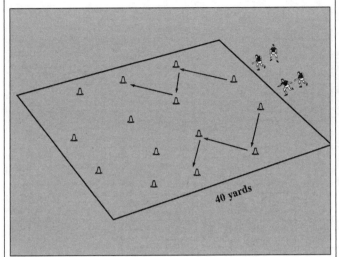

Defending Session

Organization
Players line up one behind each other at starting cone. One at a time they run forward and complete the circuit of markers. They react at each marker to the coach's command.

Commands
- Show inside
- Show outside
- Show on command

Key Factors
- Good body position
- Get side on and low to the ground
- Arc angle of run to the marker as if defending an opponent

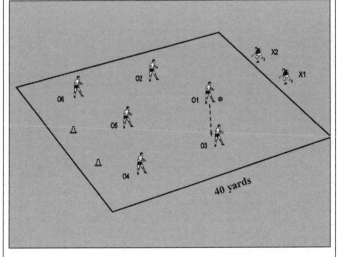

Defending Session

Organization
O1 through to O6 line up as shown in diagram. X1 and X2 work together. The ball is passed amongst O team and the ball is held after each pass. X's close down player with the ball, with one X pressuring the ball and the other X taking a covering position

Progression(s)
- O's must pass four passes minimum
- O's have two touch only
- Introduce X3 to provide balance

Key Factors
- Quickly press the ball carrier
- Cover and support - good communication
- Cover player calls - inside/outside

Defending Session

Organization
A goalkeeper, a back four and two midfielders line up against eight attacking players, using just over half a field. Balls are served into the attackers who play to goal. Defenders pressure and cover accordingly and attempt to clear balls back to server.

Progression(s)
• Add small goals for defending team to attack towards

Key Factors - Defending Principles
• Marking space for midfield trying to stop balls into strikers
• If ball is out wide - can we stop the cross?
• Communication - especially from the goalkeeper

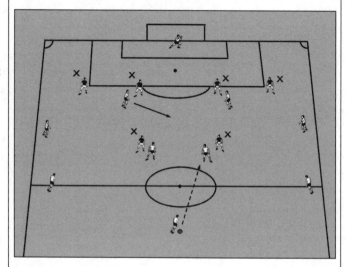

Defending Session

Organization
Similar set up as previous now with a back three and four midfielders playing against eight attackers. Balls are served in from the center circle to wide midfielders and defenders play accordingly.

Progression(s)
• Add more attackers once balls are served in
• Add a retreating forward to help cover back

Key Factors
• Communication is vital
• Pressure - Cover - Balance
• Understand individual and team responsibilities

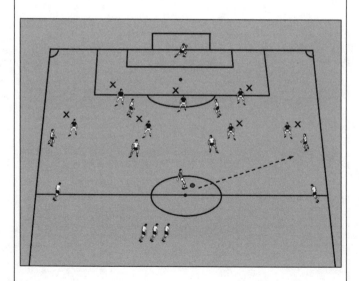

Technical Coaching Sessions

Diagram	Organization

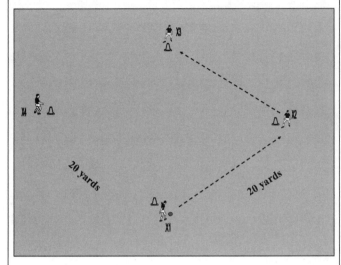

Crossing Session

Organization - Send & Push
Players in groups of fours in a 20 by 20 yard grid with each player in a corner. Each player receives, controls and passes the ball to the next player in the grid.

Progression(s)
- Have players change direction and spots in the grid
- Introduce a second ball
- Play a give-and-go, then pass to a new third corner

Key Factors
- Vary passes to next player - air, driven, bent etc
- First touch should push the ball towards target
- Square body up with target - make sure hips are facing target
- Communication and accuracy of each pass

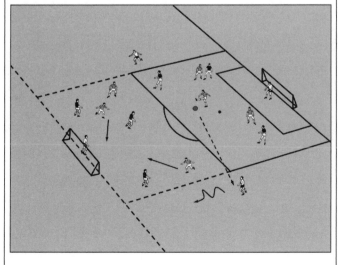

Crossing Session

Organization
On a 50 by 40 yard field play 6 v 6 with two neutral players in wide zones and goalkeepers. Adjust field dimensions or number of players if necessary. Neutral players cannot be challenged. Goals can only be scored from a cross.

Progression(s)
- Neutral players have a time limit in which to serve the ball
- Players who pass to neutral player must switch positions with them

Key Factors
- Play to neutral player as early as possible
- Vary delivery into goal area - high, low
- Vary distance from crosses - end line or half way line

Technical Coaching Sessions

Crossing Session

Organization
Two lines of players 40 yards from goal. X2 pass ball down line for X1 to run onto and cross. First player from O line runs into goal area to score from cross.

Progression(s)
- X1 and X2 play give and go to start sequence
- Add second attacker
- Add a defender

Key Factors
- Accelerate down line with head up looking at target player
- Drive crosses hard and low to front post
- Loft balls in air to back post

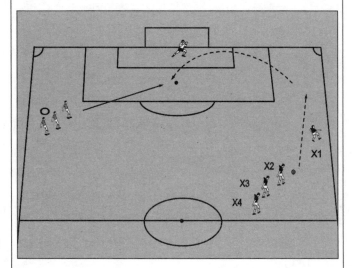

Crossing Session

Organization
Three groups of four play with two groups against one. Grid size is approximately 35 yards by 15 yards. Two groups at either end with defending team in the middle. Team X tries to play the ball through or over middle groups (O) grid. O's can then send one player at a time to other grid to win the ball from X team.

Progression(s)
- Add keepers into any grid

Key Factors
- Accuracy of cross
- Height of cross
- Does the cross go through or over?

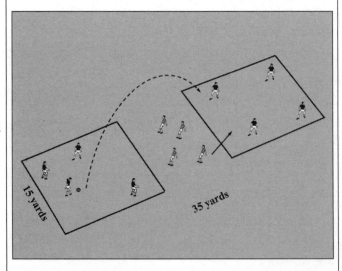

Diagram	Organization

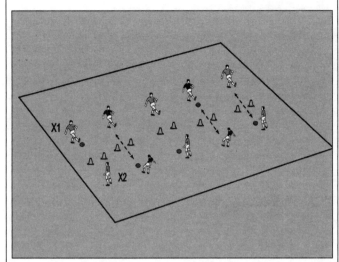

Shooting & Finishing Session

Organization
In pairs players strike the ball back to each other through the cones.

Progression(s)
• Vary distance apart
• One touch or two touch

Key Factors
• Head down over the ball
• Ankle lock with toe down
• Planted foot next to the ball
• Striking the ball with the laces

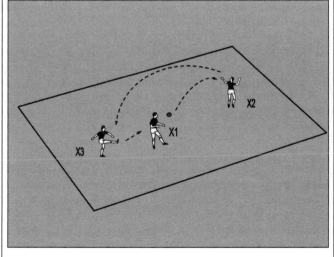

Shooting & Finishing Session

Organization
In threes using one ball. X1 tosses ball to X2 who heads the ball over to X3. X3 then volleys the ball back to X1 so that X1 can catch the ball.

Progression(s)
• Rotate all positions

Key Factors
• Header must be with mouth closed, eyes on the ball and a defensive header (up and away)
• X3 must adjust to the flight of the ball
• left foot, right foot.

Chapter Two

Functional Sessions

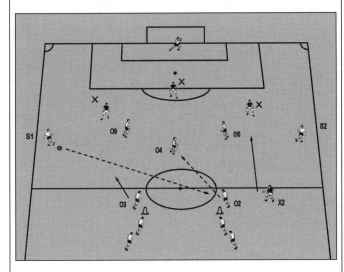

Counter Attacking

Organization
S1 plays ball into O2, who controls and plays ball into O4. As the pass from O2 goes forward X2 can make recovery run, to create a 5 v 4 situation. Repeat other way with S2 playing into O3 who then plays forward to X4. His partner O2 also joins in.

Progression(s)
• Rotate all positions
• Restrict touches

Key Factors
• Movement - with and without the ball
• Quality of pass
• Receiving qualities of O2/O3/O4

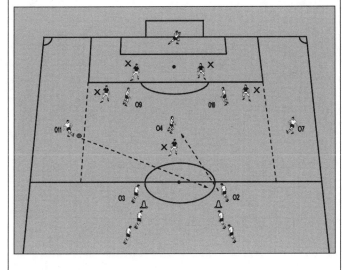

Counter Attacking

Organization
Similar set up as previous. O11 plays ball into O2 who plays into O4, to create a 5 v 5 situation. Objective to try and attack centrally, but if defence is narrow, play wide to O7 or O11.

Progression(s)
• Rotate all positions
• Allow defence to play out to target goals/player

Key Factors
• Movement of front players
• Quality of pass
• Support play - in advance or behind
• Decisions - speed of attack, point of attack

Counter Attacking

Organization
X1 plays the ball across to X3. O7 intercepts and plays forward early to O9. On first touch X3 makes recovery run creating a 3 v 2 situation. Repeat from both sides with X2 starting by passing towards X4.

Progression(s)
• Rotate all positions

Key Factors
• Good first touch from attacking midfielders after interception
• Hold up play from O9 - must maintain possession
• Try to play in support player to create goalscoring opportunity

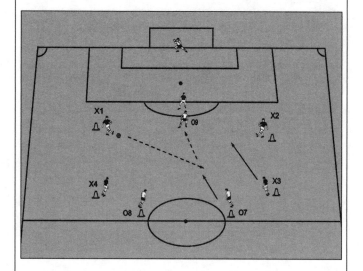

Counter Attacking

Organization
Two groups play 4 v 2 on each side of field. X's play keep away until O's win possession. Upon winning the ball, O's play into O9 and both follow creating a 3 v 1. Repeat both sides.

Progression(s)
• Introduce a recovering defender
• Add another attacker from opposite group

Key Factors
• Speed of play - attack with purpose
• Move single defender out of middle

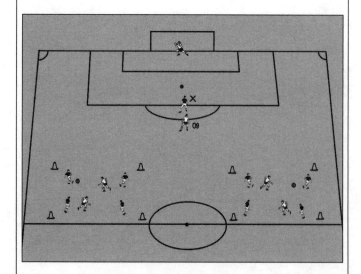

Functional Coaching Sessions

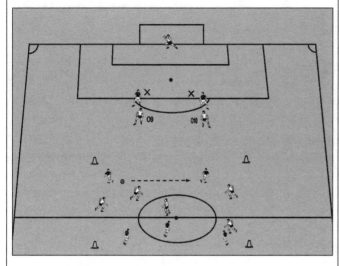

Counter Attacking

Organization

Two teams of five play in the middle area of the field. X's try and keep ball. When O's win possession they play forward to O9 or O10. At least two O players assist O9 and O10 creating a 4 v 2 situation.

Progression(s)

• Allow a recovering defender to create 4 v 3

Key Factors

• Forwards must maintain possession
• Overlaps and cross-overs to move defenders around
• Attack with purpose and at speed

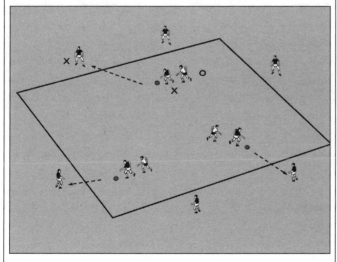

Counter Attacking

Organization

In a 25 by 30 yard grid, 6 players on the outside with three team mates in the middle and three defenders marking them. X's on outside play ball in and O's defend passively. X's in the middle turn and play ball out.

Progression(s)

• Rotate and reverse all roles

Key Factors

• Vary turns and passes in and out
• Set and turn with and without the ball
• All central players must get a touch before playing out
• Good communication and movement

Functional Coaching Sessions

Counter Attacking

Organization
X1 plays into X2. O defends. Use supporting players on the sides to maintain possession. Reverse roles. Grid size can vary depending on age and ability.

Progression(s)
• Supporting players play one or two touch
• Rotate all positions

Key Factors
• Look at how X1 receives the ball - behind, side, front - creation of space

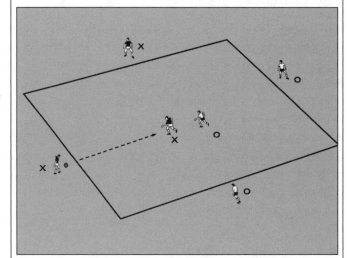

Counter Attacking

Organization
Similar set up as previous using a slightly larger grid. X plays into X1 or X2 and then joins in to create a 3 v 2 situation. Play keep away until ball is intercepted and then reverse roles. Supporting players on outside of grid are restricted to two touch.

Progression(s)
• Supporting players now play one touch

Key Factors
• Defenders must close down quickly and deny space
• Look for attackers to:
   - create space
   - variety of turns
   - combination play

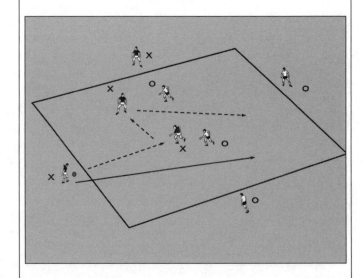

Functional Coaching Sessions

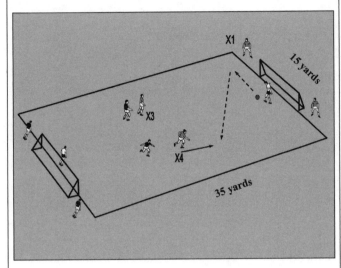

Counter Attacking

Organization

GK passes ball to X1 or X2. Within two touches X1 plays infield to X3 or X4. Both X1 and X2 join in creating a 4 v 2 situation. O's defend accordingly. X's attack to score past opposing GK. Field dimensions can vary with ability and age of players.

Progression(s)
- Repeat the other way
- Allow only one support attacker creating a 3 v 2

Key Factors
- Look for quality of pass infield
- Look for creation of space by front two
- Look for types of turns with/without the ball
- Look for combination play

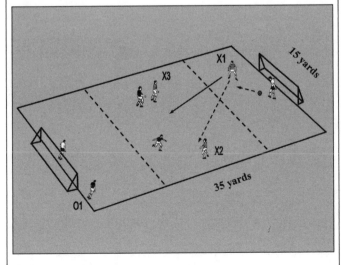

Counter Attacking

Organization

GK plays ball into X1. X2 and X3 must start in the middle zone. X1 plays forward and joins in creating a 3 v 2. Use a 35 by 15 yard game field.

Progression(s)
- Repeat the other way with O1 coming in and X1 dropping out
- Rotate all positions
- Develop to 3 v 3 but O1 starts in defending third

Key Factors
- Look for X1 opening out
- How do forwards create space
- Supporting runs - when and where?
- Try and get in behind with timed runs and correct passes

Functional Coaching Sessions

Switching The Play

Organization
Players line up in positions as allocated by cones from one goal area to the other. Players pass and follow pass to next position. Two groups working, one going in one direction and the other team moving in the opposite direction.

Progression(s)
• Use more than one ball
• Play one or two touch

Key Factors
• Good first touch out of feet
• Look to "open up" early
• Get side on when receiving the ball

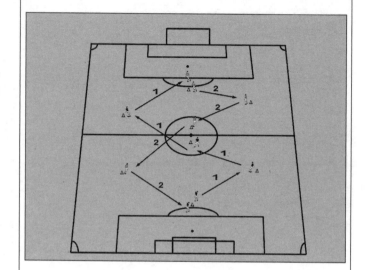

Switching The Play

Organization
Starting at half field, X5 plays into X9 or X10. X9 or X10 sets back to X4 or X8 to control and play to wide players X7 or X11. Once ball is played to wide player, overlap to create a 2 v 1 out wide. Take on wide defender and cross into middle for forwards to attack and score.

Progression(s)
• Rotate all positions

Key Factors
• Allow players to be creative and play as they see it
• Support runs after passes

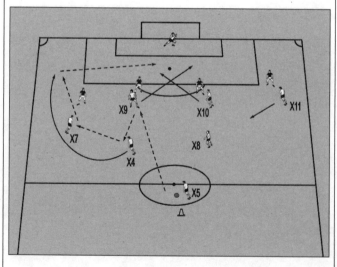

Functional Coaching Sessions

Diagram	Organization

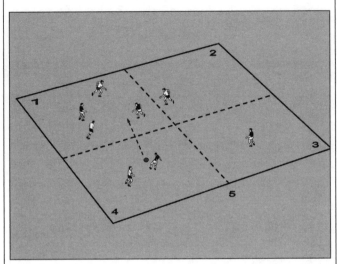

Switching The Play

Organization
A 30 by 20 yard grid is divided into 5 areas, the fifth being the complete grid itself. Two teams of four play regular keep away in the grid that the coach calls out.

Progression(s)
- Open possession
- Time possession
- Unlimited touches/progress to two touch

Key Factors
- Individual ability to maintain possession
- Quality of passes
- Team must achieve set number of passes
- Good ball control

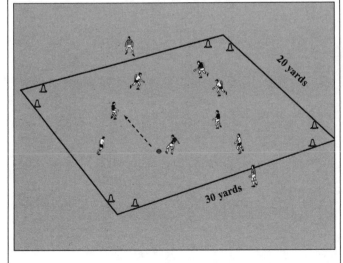

Switching The Play

Organization
On a 30 by 20 yard field two teams play 4 v 4 with neutral target players on each side of the 30 yard side. Four small goals are placed in the corners of the field. Teams must score having switched through a target player.

Progression(s)
- Add a third team to play on and off (to increase speed of play)
- Rotate target players

Key Factors
- Quality of passing
- Good ball control
- Speed of play
- Support and balance
- Movement of players
- Communication
- Shielding

Organization	Diagram

Switching The Play

Organization
Two teams of eight or more players play with five players on the field with others waiting to join in. Each team has a goalkeeper and play always starts with the goalkeeper throwing the ball out to a team mate. The field size will depend on the number of players on the field. Players must play through small wide goals/cones before going to goal.

Progression(s)
• Add/reduce players
• Add a second ball

Key Factors
• Rotate players in and out so the teams always have to adjust
• Possession must have a purpose (direction to achieve topic example: score)
• Team understanding
• Balance and support
• Switch the ball quickly after playing through wide goals

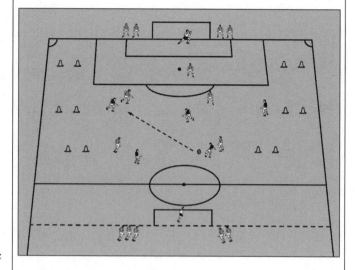

Switching The Play

Organization
Two teams play 4 v 4 or 5 v 5 with goalkeepers. Each game starts with the goalkeeper. Teams play to score but must maintain possession for certain number of passes first.

Progression(s)
• All players must touch the ball before team can score
• One team must score within five touches, other team must score after five touches

Key Factors
• Quality of passing
• Supporting runs
• Good team balance

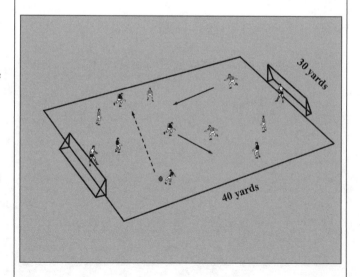

Functional Coaching Sessions

Diagram	Organization

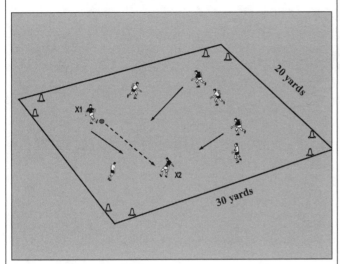

Improving Transition

Organization
On a 30 by 20 yard field with multiple goals, two teams of four play with open possession.

Progression(s)
- Add a third team to rotate in and out

Key Factors
- Communication
- Longer passes
- Team understanding
- X1 plays balls to X2 and the whole teams moves to support X2
- Work on transition of play from one goal to the next
- Move and work as a unit

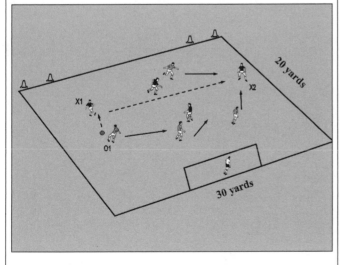

Improving Transition

Organization
Teams play 5 v 5 plus a goalkeeper. Team X attacks the large goal and goalkeeper where team O defends and they counter into small goals at opposite end.

Progression(s)
- Limit touches on the ball
- Time possession game

Key Factors
- O1 has lost possession of the ball to X1. X1 passes to X2 and the O team all react from attacking to defending
- Team shape and balance
- The X team changes to attacking mentality quickly and attack with purpose

Speed Of Play

Organization
A 30 by 25 yard grid is split in half. Each team X and O has five players. Attacking team X starts with ball on their side of grid and O send in two defenders to win it back. Once it is won, the defenders rejoin their team mates and the X team sends two defenders to win ball back.

Progression(s)
• Two defenders may enter other half
• Three defenders may enter other half
• Two touch play only

Key Factors
• Get big early - heels on lines, body open to field
• Receive ball with back leg
Always know your next pass before you receive the ball

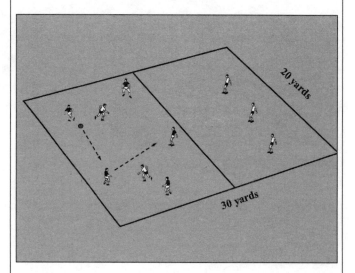

Speed Of Play

Organization
Two teams play 7 v 7 to wide goals. Each team defends two wide goals. A middle channel is marked where players are restricted to two touches only in that zone.

Progression(s)
• Add two neutral players creating a 9 v 7 situation

Key Factors
• Play quickly through center channel
• Identify and solve 2 v 1
• Stay away from pressure pockets

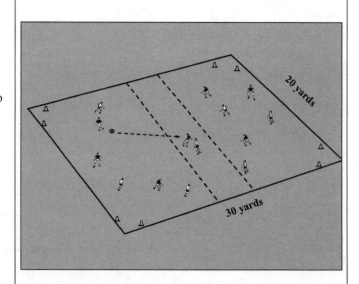

Diagram	Organization

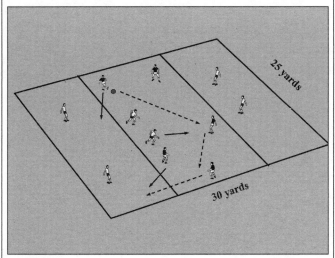

Support Play

Organization
A 30 by 25 yard grid split into three zones. Five X players pass the ball around the two O players. Once they have completed five passes they move to the next zone.

Progression(s)
• Two touch only
• Rotate positions

Key Factors
• Players aware of team shape
• Speed of play
• Options of support
• Team shape

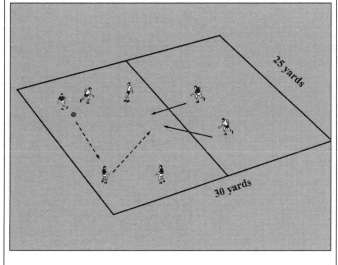

Support Play

Organization
The same 30 by 25 yard grid is now split in half. Teams play 4 v 4 possession. All players must be inside grid to achieve point.

Progression(s)
• Set number of passes for goal
• Two touch only

Key Factors
• Game speed
• Communication
• Look for one or two touch soccer

Support Play

Organization
Teams play 7 v 7 with one team defending a large goal and the other team defending two small goals. Each game starts with goalkeeper distributing the ball out.

Progression(s)
• Rotate teams so both are attacking large/small goals
• Two touch only

Key Factors
• Team understanding - what is good support play?
• Movement to support ball carrier
• Movement away to create space, which creates a passing opportunity to relieve pressure on the ball carrier

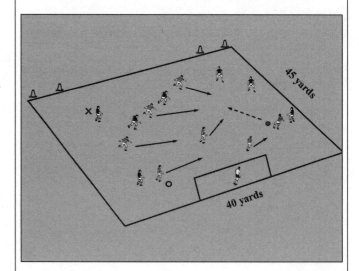

Support Play

Organization
Full field regular 11 v 11 game. Regular rules apply.

Progression(s)
• Reduce touches on the ball

Key Factors
• Look for correct team shape
• Support - with or without the ball
• Show to feet - don't always run away
• Maintain possession - start again if needs be
• Do not always look to play forward - draw opponents out

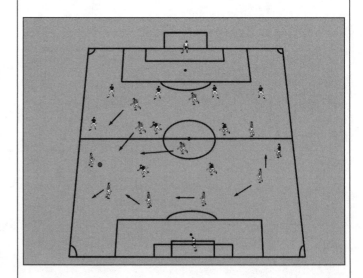

| Diagram | Organization |

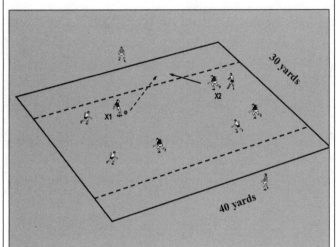

Depth In Attack

Organization
Two teams of four play to target players on a 40 by 30 yard field. The field is marked with zones at each end in which players must receive ball in before they go to target player. X1 passes to X2. X2 must receive the ball in the attacking area before playing into target

Progression(s)
• Rotate all positions
• Two touch only
• One touch into target player

Key Factors
• Attacking players can not be in attacking area until the ball is played to the area (through ball) - offside rule is in effect
• Look for separation
• Speed of play
• Timing of run and through ball
• Communication - not always verbal (eye contact, pointing, etc.)

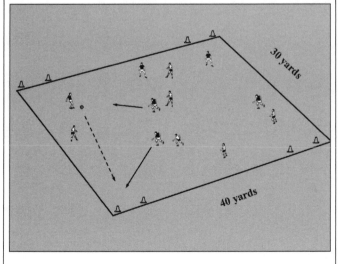

Depth In Attack

Organization
On the same sized 40 by 30 yard field, two teams of six now play to counter goals. X1 plays a line ball to X2. This shows how you can gain field advantage in one pass.

Progression(s)
• Two touch

Key Factors
• Look to eliminate players with the pass
• Look for driven pass
• Movement off the ball
• Be patient
• Look to play into running players
• Maintain team shape while committing to attack and creating space

Functional Coaching Sessions

Width In Attack

Organization
Two teams of six play within a 40 by 25 yard grid. No tackling permitted (shadow play). Two wide zones where a player from each team can stand. Both teams play to opposite ends of the field. A player from either team must receive the ball in the wide zone before they go to end line. They then turn and attack opposite line.

Progression(s)
- Rotate positions
- Play two touch
- Tackling permitted

Key Factors
- Speed of play
- Get wide as quick as possible
- X1 plays to X2. X2 has given width to the play and can now play into X3. X3 then dribbles to end line.

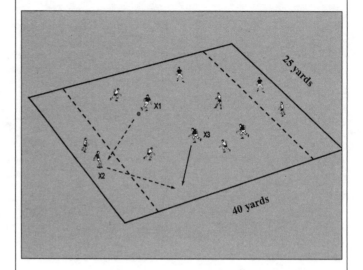

Width In Attack

Organization
Teams play 6 v 6 with 2 neutral players. The neutrals play for team in possession. The game is played on a field 50 by 35 yards in dimension with one large goal and two small goals at opposite end.

Progression(s)
- Rotate so both teams attack in each direction
- Play two touch

Key Factors
- Speed of play
- Spread the play wide
- Quality of ball - play wide or into feet centrally
- Driven, lofted or swerve passes
- Do not be predictable in play

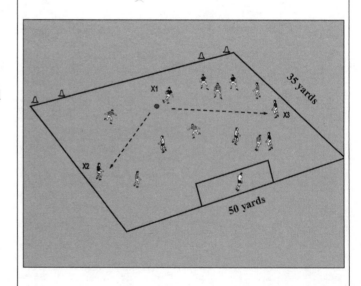

Functional Coaching Sessions

Diagram	Organization

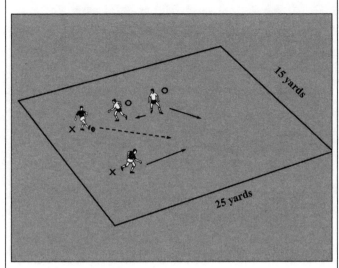

Defending 2 v 2

Organization
In a grid size 25 by 15 yards, play 2 v 2 keep ball.

Progression(s)
• Add direction by scoring a point for taking ball from end
  line to end line
• Add goals for players to score in

Key Factors
• Pressure/cover support
• Proper space between defenders 1 and 2
• Communication
• Correct side of support
• Isolate forward
• Defend with your back to goal

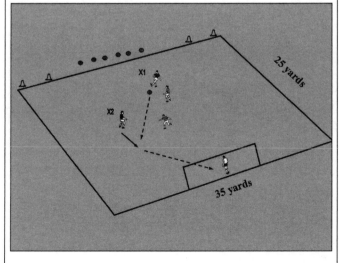

Defending 2 v 2

Organization
On a slightly larger field 35 by 25 yards, play 2 v 2 with
a goalkeeper. One team attacks the large goal with the
goalkeeper while the defending team has two small targets to
dribble/pass through. There are a supply of balls at end line
between two small targets with which to restart with after
breakdown/goal.

Progression(s)
• Rotate all positions
• Players to perform in set time period (i.e. unlimited touches
  for five minutes)

Key Factors
• Deny penetration
• Deny shots on goal
• Push player with ball away from goal
• Regain possession
• Count number of breakdowns

Organization	Diagram

Defending 3 v 3

Organization
On a 30 by 20 yard grid play 3 v 3 keep away.

Progression(s)
• Progress to scoring by stopping ball on end line
• Progress to scoring in small goals

Key Factors
• Responsibilities - O1 pressure, O2 Support/cover, O3 balance
• Communication
• Be aware of X's movement off the ball
• Look for numbers up situation
• Individual patience - don't dive in or sell yourself

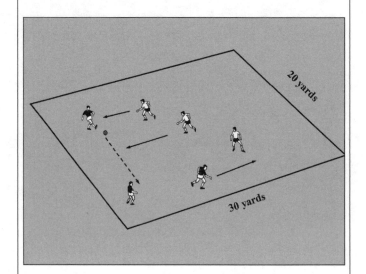

Defending 3 v 3

Organization
Play 3 v 3 plus goalkeepers on a 35 by 25 yard field with two large goals at each end.

Progression(s)
• Play two touch
• If defending team wins possession, they have to start back with goalkeeper before attacking opposite end

Key Factors
• Correct support from team mates
• Communication must be loud, clear and positive
• Role of goalkeeper as a "sweeper-keeper"

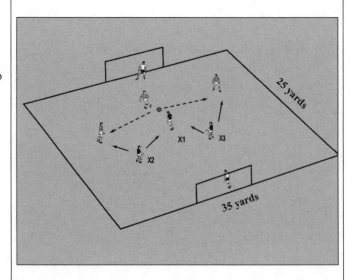

Functional Coaching Sessions

Diagram	Organization

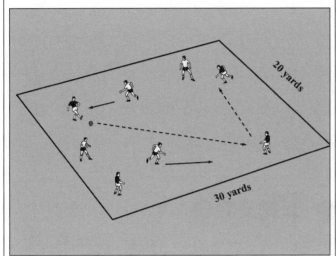

High Pressure

Organization
On a 30 by 25 yard grid, two teams of four play keep away. Team in possession must try and get eight consecutive passes to get a point.

Progression(s)
- Add a neutral player to play on attacking team only
- Play two touch

Key Factors
- Immediate pressure
- High communication
- Physical presence

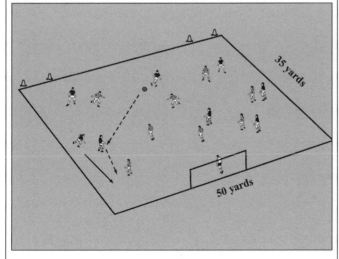

High Pressure

Organization
Team X attacks the large goal which team O defends. Two teams of eight play on a larger 50 by 30 yard field. X must achieve a set number of shots in a set time. O must maintain possession or counter in small goal at opposite ends.

Progression(s)
- Rotate teams shooting directions

Key Factors
- X team pushing forward
- 1 v 1 tactics
- Crosses
- After a shot or goal, O team can play out of the back
- Add pressure to a team by making them a goal down
- Can players motivate each other?

Chapter Three

Tactical Sessions

Diagram	Organization

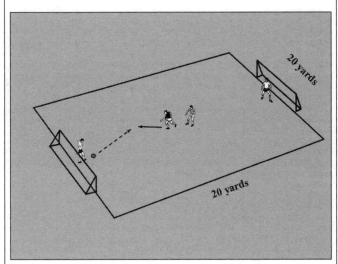

Individual Attacking Behavior

Organization
Players play 1 v 1 with all time goalkeepers. Goalkeeper plays ball into forward who has checked off his defender. Attacker receives ball and controls, dribbles and tries to score past opposing defender and goalkeeper. Passive defending to begin with.

Progression(s)
• Progress to active defending and counter attacking
• Rotate positions

Key Factors
• Quality of pass into attacker
• Good first touch
• Positive - take defender on
• Use variety of moves - don't be predictable

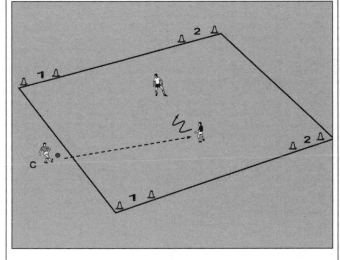

Individual Attacking Behavior

Organization
On a 20 by 20 yard grid with goals in each corner - the coach serves to attacker who controls and then dribbles into defenders half of the field. On coaches command 1 or 2, the forward reacts by trying to score in that numbered goal

Progression(s)
• Rotate positions
• Allow forwards to decide which goal to score in

Key Factors
• Speed of play - react quickly to coaches command
• Good first touch

Organization	Diagram

Individual Attacking Behavior

Organization
Two teams play together in two different halves. Player X gets the ball from the goalkeeper. Attacker X in the second half of the field gets away from the defender and calls for the ball. Upon receiving the ball they then attempt to outplay the defender and shoot.

Progression(s)
- Rotate all positions
- Passive defending becoming more active

Key Factors
- Encourage being comfortable in possession
- Good first touch
- Play with head up
- Attack at speed
- Creativity and positive attitude - don't be afraid to take risks in the attacking third

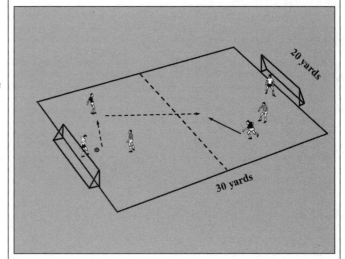

Individual Attacking Behavior

Organization
Four players are numbered and are placed around the outside of the field each with a ball. Two players wait in the middle. The coach calls a number who serves in their ball. First player on the ball becomes the attacker, the other one defender. If the ball is served from 1 or 3, the player has to attack goal 2. If the ball comes from 2 or 4, goal 1 must be attacked.

Progression(s)
- Add goalkeepers to defend goals
- Rotate all positions

Key Factors
- Be alert and ready
- Anticipation - up on toes
- Attack the ball
- Switch on quickly - which goal to attack

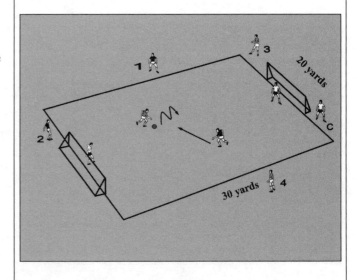

Diagram	Organization

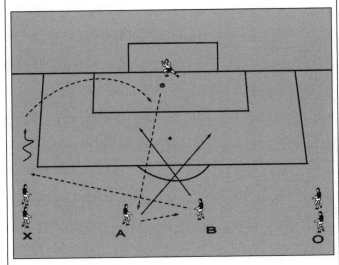

Effective Attacking Behavior

Organization
The goalkeeper throws the ball to player A. A lays off to player B who drives a diagonal ball to the left flank to player X. Player X crosser the ball after short ball control. Players A and B move into the penalty area interchanging their positions.

Progression(s)
- Repeat both sides with GK throwing to player B
- Rotate all positions

Key Factors
- Players cross before entering the penalty area
- Vary crosses - short, long, driven, lofted
- Timing and angles of attacking runs
- Type of finish
- Composure

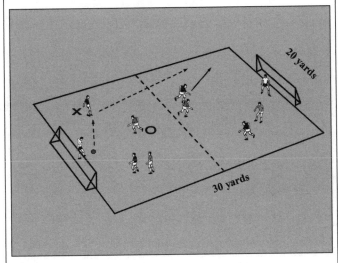

Effective Attacking Behavior

Organization
Two team play 4 v 4 on an appropriate game field. Each team must play with two players in each half. Players have to pass the ball from the defending zone into the attacking zone. Their teammates have to outplay the defenders and finish off.

Progression(s)
- Players rotate positions and partners
- Add in a neutral player to be an all-time attacker creating a 3 v 2 situation

Key Factors
- Get free from the defenders
- Create passing opportunities
- Accurate passing and shooting
- Wall passes, cross-overs etc

Team Shape - Playing Out From The Back

Organization
Goalkeeper and defenders (X) line up in regular positions. The ball is played into the goalkeeper who catches. Defenders create space. GK throws ball out to one of the defenders. Defending player receives and runs the ball over the end line.

Progression(s)
- Use all players
- GK to use feet only

Key Factors
- Create space quickly - spread out to maximise individual space
- Delivery from GK - throw to feet or space?
- Receiving body position
- Forward thinking/forward moving
- Position of players without the ball - supporting/covering

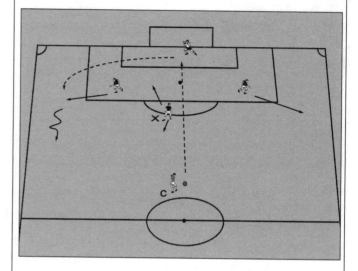

Team Shape - Playing Out From The Back

Organization
Same set up as previous but with an attacker (O) now included. The ball is played into the GK who catches. The attacker chooses a defender to close down. GK throws to unmarked defender. Once the ball is thrown out, attacker must stop defenders getting the ball to end line.

Progression(s)
- Add a second attacker

Key Factors
- Can the player in possession "get out"?
- If they can not - work on appropriate turning technique, support of other players, communication between players
- Can another player "get out"?

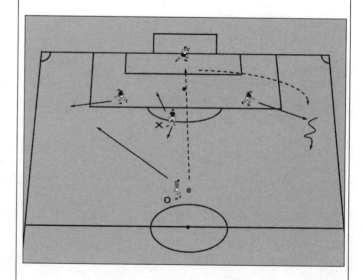

Tactical Coaching Sessions

Diagram	Organization

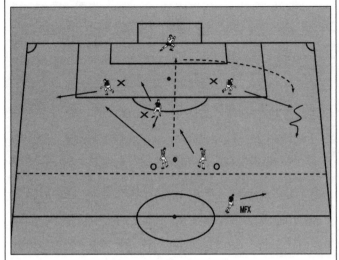

Team Shape - Playing Out From The Back

Organization
Same set up as previous but now with a defending midfielder (MFX) as a target player. Ball is played into GK who throws out to an unmarked defender. Attackers pressure the defenders. Defenders must get ball to MFX.

Progression(s)
- MFX to get closed down once they receive ball
- Defenders to help midfielder with supporting run/overlap
- Add a MFO to defend against MFX

Key Factors
- Supporting position of midfielder
- Receiving body position of midfielder
- Runs to assist midfielder

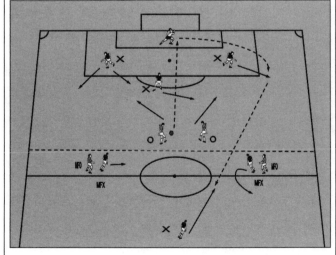

Team Shape - Playing Out from The Back

Organization
Same set up as previous but now with two MFX's and two MFO's and an attacker X. The ball is played into the GK who distributes out to unmarked defender X. Defenders X combine if needed to get ball into MFX or directly into attacker X. MFX's make appropriate runs to support/complete task

Progression(s)
- Add a defender O to marker against attacker X

Key Factors
- Movement of attacker X
- Quality of passes/types of passes
- Supporting runs to assist player in possession

Organization	Diagram

Counter Attacking

Organization

In a 35 by 25 yard grid, play 4 v 4 with an all time attacker and three supporting players on outside. T1 plays ball into grid to an O player. O's try and keep possession and can play with neutral player and supporting players on outside. On coaches whistle, the o's must try and dribble over the end line or play forward into waiting O9 or O10. Two defenders mark up against forwards O9 and O10.

Progression(s)

- If X's win possession then they keep ball and play into their target players
- Allow a player to support attackers creating a 3 v 2 situation
- Rotate all positions

Key Factors

- Play three touch, two touch then one touch
- Forwards work off each other - create space

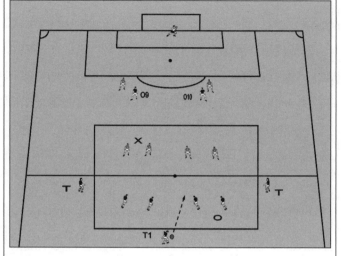

Counter Attacking

Organization

A 60 by 40 yard field is split into thirds. O plays the ball into X creating a 4 v 4 in the final third. All players stay in the third. X's must get ball into the middle third while O's close down and pressure. If O's intercept they can shoot on goal. If X's succeed then they get to dribble into middle third and they play ball into A. Repeat.

Progression(s)

- Allow one recovering defender 1 v 1
- Allow supporting attacker out 2 v 1
- Allow ball to be played into middle third for runner
- Offside applies

Key Factors

- Support player in possession
- Create space
- Take player on if 1 v 1
- When regaining possession, play with head up and transition quickly

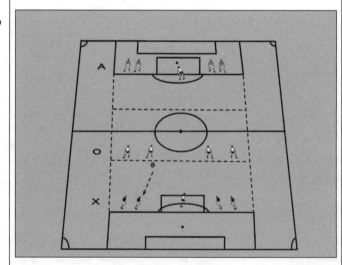

Tactical Coaching Sessions

Diagram	Organization

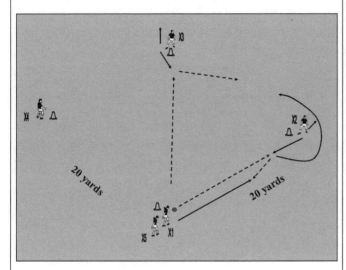

Rotational Play - Movement From Flanks

Organization
X1 passes to X2. X2 controls and sets back to X1. X2 goes down line and X3 comes short. X1 to X2 who controls and sets back. X2 runs infield and X3 comes wide. X1 to X2 who controls and sets back to X1 who plays forward to X3. X4 comes off line to set up from X3

Progression(s)
• Repeat all drills other way

Key Factors
• Play two touch
• Good first touch - side on
• Head up
• Communicate

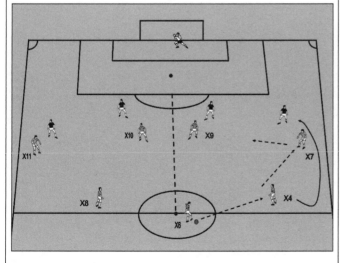

Rotational Play - Wide Positions

Organization
Using one half of the field (split down the middle) play 3 v 2. X6 plays into X4 who controls and plays wide to X7. X7 can combine with X4 and X9 to cross or shoot

Progression(s)
• Rotate both sides
• Take away center divide and bring in two central defending midfielders

Key Factors
• Encourage full back to force wide player inside/outside
• Encourage wide player to dribble and cross when in line with 18 yard area
• Look for overlap or diagonal runs from midfielder
• Look for front player to drop out
Be creative - no set formula, play as you see it

Tactical Coaching Sessions

Quality Movement Of Front Players

Organization
Using one half of a regular sized field, X8 starts by passing to X4. X4 opens out and plays wide to X7. Forwards X9 and X10 make space by switching/moving appropriately.

Progression(s)
- Wall pass between X7 and X9
- X7 plays ball down line for X9 to run on to and cross
- X7 plays into feet of X9 who turns and plays into X10's path. X10 runs on and shoots
- Repeat both sides

Key Factors
- First touch and movement infield by X7
- Movement of front two - options
- Speed and movement of player and ball
- Quality of finish

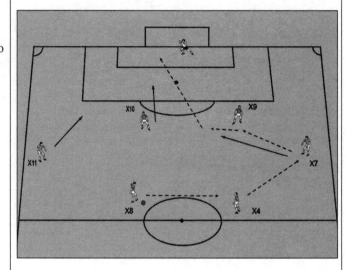

Quality Movement Of front Players

Organization
Same set up as previous with X4 passing wide to X7. X7 receives and takes ball inside. X7 plays to second striker X10 who sets up for X9 or X7 (who has continued run) to shoot.

Progression(s)
- X7 plays to X9 and overlaps and shoots. X10 runs in for rebounds
- X7 plays towards X9 who lets ball run to X10. X9 spins around X10 and shoots first time
- Midfielders become forwards
- Repeat both sides

Key Factors
- Movement infield by wide player
- Angle and timing of runs from front players
- Quality of pass
- End product

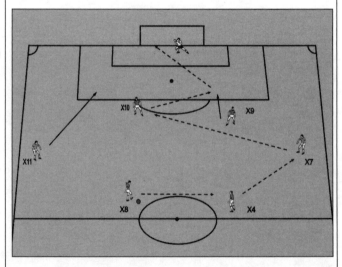

Tactical Coaching Sessions

Diagram	Organization

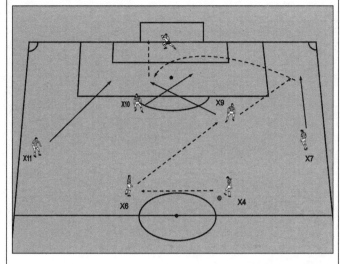

Quality Movement Of Front Players

Organization
X4 plays to X6 who in turn plays a diagonal pass to X9. X9 controls and plays ball down line for X7. X7 runs onto pass and crosses for X9, X10 and X11 to score. Rotate both sides.

Progression(s)
- X7 runs infield instead of down line and receives pass
- X9 controls and plays diagonal ball to X11 to run onto and cross

Key Factors
- Create space - angle to receive
- Quality of pass forward
- Support position behind ball
- Angle/timing of run in advance
- End product

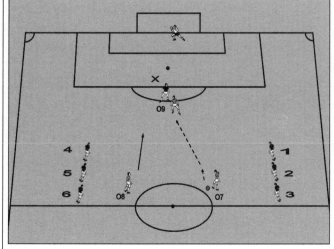

Quality Movement Of Front Players

Organization
Using half a field to attack, O7 plays out of feet and then forward to O9 who is marked by X. O8 joins in creating a 3 v 1 situation.

Progression(s)
- Include recovery run by 1, 2, 3, 4 etc - Coach calls out #

Key Factors
- Quality of pass
- Quality of receiving touch
- Support play behind/advance
- Finish

Tactical Coaching Sessions

Basic Movement Around The Box

Organization

X1 passes to X2. X2 takes one touch then passes to X3. As ball is moving to X2, X3 and X4 move away. As eye contact is made, X3 shows for the ball, receives it, plays it back to X1 and moves inside. X1 plays ball into space for X4. X4 shoots.

Progression(s)

• Rotate all positions
• Play two touch then one touch if ability allows

Key Factors

• Quality of pass
• Quality of movement
• Timing of runs
• Play with head up

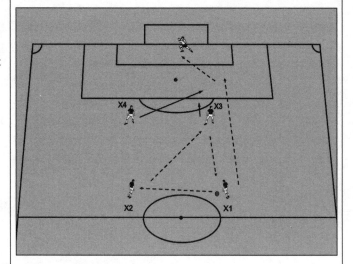

Basic Movement Around The Box

Organization

Same set up as previous. X1 passes to X2. X2 controls and plays into X3 who has checked in. X3 sets back for X1 and then spins out wide. X1 has two options: diagonal ball to X4 or ball down line to X3.

Progression(s)

• Rotate all positions

Key Factors

• Quality passes
• Quick spin out by X3
• Side on position

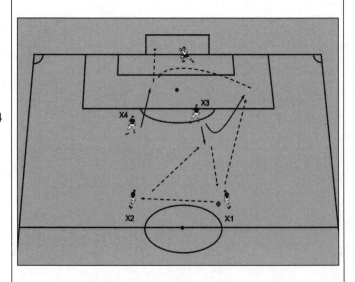

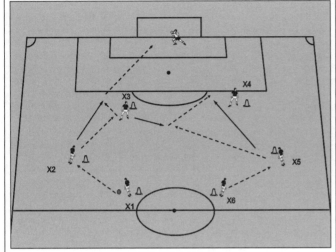

Basic Movement Around The Box

Organization
X1 passes to X2. First touch behind the cone. X3 comes off at an angle and X2 passes to X3. X3 lays ball back into X2's path for shot on goal. X6 passes to X5. First touch takes them in front of cone and pass to X3. X3 receives on back foot and lays off for X5 to shoot.

Progression(s)
• Repeat both sides
• Rotate all positions

Key Factors
• Quality of receiving touch
• Good lay-off by X3
• Timing of runs - run onto the ball to shoot

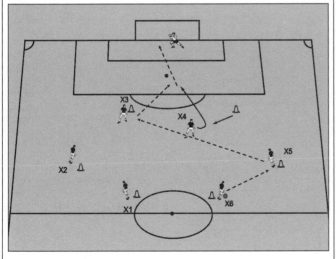

Basic Movement Around The Box

Organization
X6 passes to X5 who controls the ball behind the cone and passes to X4. X3 gives a shout "over". X4 leaves ball to X3 and spins away. X3 lays ball off to X4 who shoots.

Progression(s)
• Repeat other side
• Rotate positions

Key Factors
• Timing of call "over"
• Timing of run
• Side on position

Tactical Coaching Sessions

Organization	Diagram

Receiving In The Middle & Attacking Third

Organization
GK throws ball into middle third. Defending team allow first touch then press. Play through midfield and then into the front players. One midfielder can join in attacking third without being tracked. Otherwise everyone stays in their zonal areas. If pressured, midfielders can play back to defensive third or off O7 and O11 who return ball back on two touch.

Progression(s)
• Repeat both ways
• Rotate all positions
• When ball is played back to defenders O2 or O3, they look to switch to either O11 or O7 who then cross for O9 and O10

Key Factors
• Create space prior to receiving
• Midfield shape - not flat
• Quality of pass into midfield
• Type of control
• Composure - relax under pressure

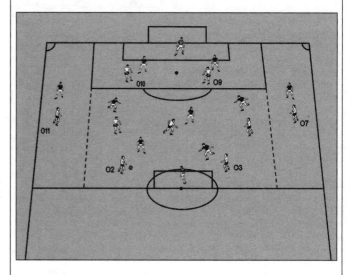

Receiving In The Middle & Attacking Third

Organization
S1 plays ball into O2 who controls and plays ball into O4. As the pass from O2 goes forward, X2 can make recovery run to create a 5 v 4 situation.

Progression(s)
• Repeat the other way with S2 playing into O3 who then plays forward to O4.
• Use servers S1 and S2 into attack as wide players

Key Factors
• Receiving qualities of O2/O3/O4
• Movement of front players
• Quality of pass
• Support play - in advance or in behind
• Decisions - speed/point of attack

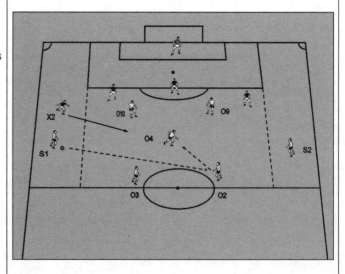

Diagram	Organization

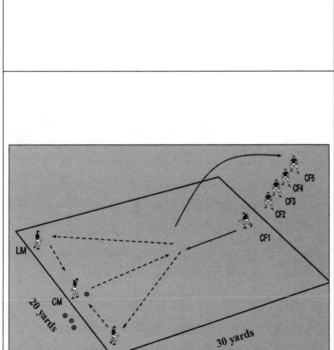

Set Up Play

Organization

Using a 20 x 30-yard area with eight players, three players position themselves as midfielders, left midfield (LM), central midfield (CM) and right midfield (RM). All other players position in a line opposite the CM, 30 yards away. These are the center forwards (CF)

CF1 drops deep at an angle to the left or right to receive a pass from CM. CM plays into CF and CF plays ball to the midfielder on that side of the square. LM/RM plays back to CM. CF spins out and joins back of line. CF 2 continues drill by dropping short and continue.

Progression(s)
- Play one touch passing
- Rotate all positions

Key Factors
- CF must come short for the pass quickly and at an angle
- CF after dropping ball back to outside midfielders should spin as if going to goal and look for return pass
- RM/LM must be on toes and ready to play one touch to CM to keep drill moving

Set Up Play

Organization

Same set up as previous exercise but CM plays straight pass now to CF who drops short at pace. CM now shouts left or right making the CF make a split decision on who to pass to. If they call left - must play left footed across the body to LM - call right and right footed across the body to RM. Spin after pass. LM/RM to play one touch back to CM and continue with CF2.

Progression(s)
- Rotate all positions
- Play one touch passing

Key Factors
- Quick show for pass from CF
- CM shouts left or right as ball arrives at CF making them make a split second decision
- CF must adjust body quickly playing with furthest foot across their body to opposite outside midfielder
- LM/RM play back one touch quickly and accurately to CM to maintain pace of drill

Organization	Diagram

Set Up Play

Organization
Same set up as before but now with a defender (DF) putting pressure on CF. CF1 drops short to the side for pass from CM. Now second player in line acts as a DF. Allow defender to increase pressure on the attacker.

Progression(s)
• Increase pressure accordingly to full pressure defending

Key Factors
• CF must work hard to create space away from DF - when they receive pass, use body to shield the ball and play with furthest foot
• CF needs to set back to outside MF at good pace and accurately and the spin quickly as if going to goal
• DF shackles CF all the way making them have to be quick, accurate and as game like as possible

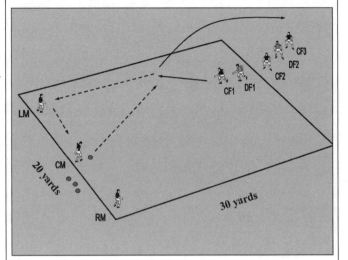

Set Up Play

Organization
Same set up as previous drills. CF drops short to one side for pass from CM. CF plays one touch back to LM. LM now plays forward into space created by CF and RM makes late run into space down their line to receive. RM returns ball to CM and drill continues with CF2.

Progression(s)
• Repeat using both flanks
• Rotate all positions
• Add defender when quality allows

Key Factors
• Pace and accuracy of pass is now paramount, especially in set up pass from CF and switch ball from LM to RM
• Timing of run from RM to receive pass must be later so as not to "fill" space created by CF
• CF should spin out down left channel which leaves right open

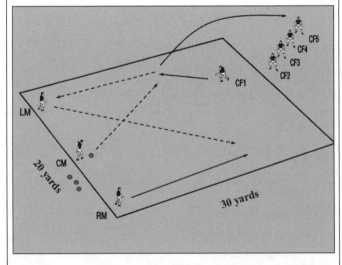

Diagram	Organization

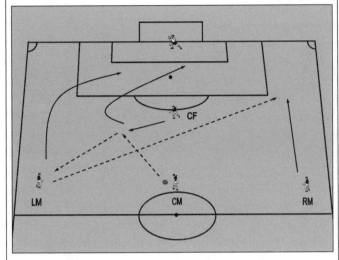

Set Up Play

Organization
Similar set up as previous exercises but now on a larger scale with goal behind CF. Area can vary depending on age and ability. CF drops short and receives pass from CM. CF lays off to LM and spins to goal. LM plays forward to RM who makes late run down right side. RM delivers first time cross for CF and late run from LM.

Progression(s)
- Add a goalkeeper (GK) once movement and passing is of sufficient quality
- Add a defender if skill level allows

Key Factors
- Passing - weight and accuracy
- Movement - dynamic, creating space
- Five touches and ball should be in the goal

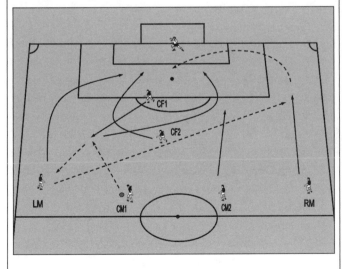

Set Up Play

Organization
Using half a field set up with two CF's, two CM's and a LM and RM as shown. CM1 passes to CF1 who in turn passes to LM. CF2 overlaps CF1 looking for pass from LM down the line but LM switches play into space as before for RM to run onto. RM crosses for CF1 and CF2 making cross over near and far post runs. CM2 and LM also make attacking runs to finish from RM's first time cross.

Progression(s)
- One touch play only
- Add a GK and DF if necessary

Key Factors
- Communication and movement between CF1 and CF2 must be good
- Timed runs and accurate well weighted passes
- One CM and one outside midfielder must attack the cross giving four options to the crosser - near, far, late and deep and penalty spot runs

Midfield Combination Play

Organization

Eight players per group line up with four players inside and four players outside a 25 x 25-yard grid. Target player (X7) passes into X's in the middle of the grid square. All four midfielders (MF) must touch the ball before playing out to another target player e.g. X5. Target player plays back into the middle and drill continues.

Progression(s)

- Play one touch for target players
- Play one touch for all players
- Rotate positions

Key Factors

- Midfielders should be on the move at all times creating good passing angles
- Target players must be alert and sliding along lines to support MF's on the ball
- Communication is vital to complete passing from one target to another in as few touches as possible

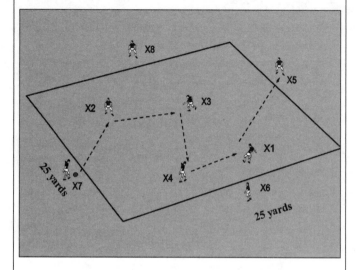

Midfield Combination Play

Organization

As before target plays to MF's X1-X4 and they combine before passing out to a target X8. X8 then plays chipped or driven through ball across to another target player X6 who plays back into supporting MF's X1-X4 first time. Drill continues,

Progression(s)

- Rotate all positions

Key Factors

- Weighted and accurate passes
- Communication
- Good supporting angles and quick combination play
- Need good set up pass for target player and weighted switch pass and play back in
- Looking for early movement of the MF's to support switched pass and set back - try and think two passes ahead and anticipate the shape of the play

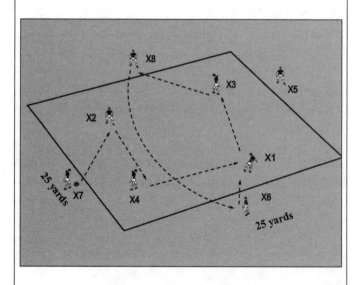

Tactical Coaching Sessions

Diagram	Organization

Midfield Combination Play

Organization

Two groups of players numbered one through six in separate squares positioned 20 yards outside the goal area. Each group passes ball between themselves and move freely in their area. One touch play if possible. Coach will randomly call out a players number and that number from each group makes an attacking MF run to goal. Each group tries to play one touch through ball for player running through who then tries to score first time. First team to score gets a point.

Progression(s)
• Bring in a GK once timing of run, combination plays, set up play and through balls are of sufficient quality.

Key Factors
• Play one touch where possible
• Create good passing angles in the midfield area
• Play with your head up and know your next pass before you receive the ball to keep speed of play quick
• Be aware of attacking MF's run and try to set up the play before passing to the runner - Do not force an unnatural pass

Midfield Combination Play

Organization

Same set up as previous drill but now with one large 25 x 50-yard grid with teams intermingling with each other. Both teams pass their own balls but under more difficult, game like situations. Now coach touches a player on the shoulder instead of calling their number so MD's have to be watching for any of their team mates attacking runs and still try to play quickly to them for them to score.

Progression(s)
• Add a defender

Key Factors
• As before but more emphasis on playing with their head up as "call" is not made
• Runner at first cannot communicate physically or verbally with team mates - players then have to recognise the moment to play forward and execute accordingly
• Quality and accuracy of passes - especially through balls

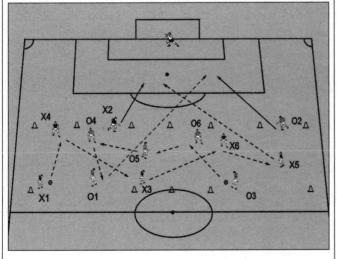

Tactical Coaching Sessions

Organization	Diagram

Defending From Free Kicks

Organization
A supply of balls are positioned around the penalty area. The center forward (CF) and goalkeeper (GK) line up the wall consisting of the four midfielders. The right full back (RFB) is positioned on the far post allowing GK to take up a central position. The best defenders, usually center backs (CB) and the left full back (LFB) mark up man for man. The other CF lines up at the edge of the box. Coach calls to attacking players which ball to work from and see how quickly the defense can get organized.

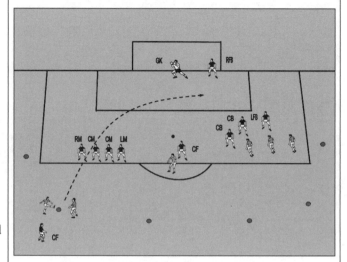

Key Factors
- Everyone must know their role
- GK and CF must stop quick takes and organize quickly and effectively
- Midfielders must maintain game shape within the wall and always form the wall. Call a CF in if the GK needs five players in the wall
- Be alert and expect the unexpected

Defending From Corners

Organization
The defending team positions themselves with RFB and LFB on each post. Which ever side the corner is taken from, that outside midfielder stands at the edge of the six yard area to clear a low driven ball in. CB's and CM's are marked up man for man with the opposite outside mid staying deep on their side for a long over hit corner. Forwards stay up field if possible but one maybe required to drop and help if GK requests.

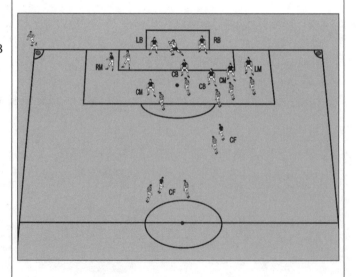

Progression(s)
- Corners kicks are taken from each side

Key Factors
- Match up height for height
- Clear the ball long, high and wide!
- Step up and out and match up as you go

Tactical Coaching Sessions

Diagram	Organization

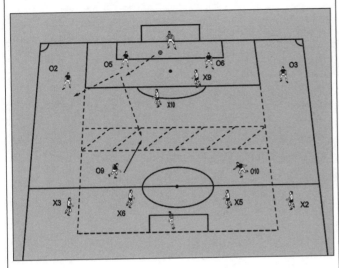

Receiving The Ball "In The Hole" To Attack

Organization
GK throws to either O5/O6. X9 and X10 can close down after first touch. O5 can either play forward to O9 or O10 or play wide to O2 or O3 who has two touches to play forward. O2 and O3 can't be challenged. One attacker O9 or O10 can come into shaded area to receive unopposed. Combine with O10 to finish 2 v 2. Repeat other way.

Progression(s)
- Allow O5 or O6 to make forward run into attacking half when the ball has gone into O9 or O10

Key Factors
- Play forward - quality and selection of pass
- Receiving qualities of the attacker in shaded area (hole)
- Combination play in attacking half
- Timing and speed of supporting runs

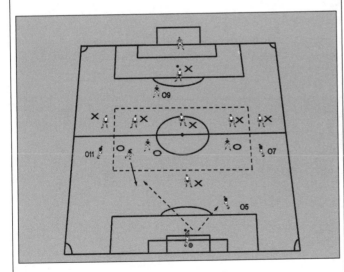

Playing Through Midfield

Organization
Teams play 8 v 8 on full or three quarter length field with a central area marked off around center circle. Play starts when GK throws to O5 or to O who has dropped out. O and O5 can combine or dribble ball into middle area. O7 and O11 can support on outside or one to join in-field for 4 v 3. Work ball into O9 with one joining in to make 2 v 1.

Progression(s)
- Rotate positions

Key Factors
- Speed of play
- Passing angles and supporting runs

Tactical Coaching Sessions

Organization

Diagram

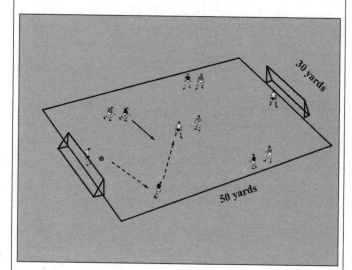

Transition/Speed Of Play

Organization
Teams play 4 v 4 with one all time attacker and GK's in each goal. Field size can vary depending on ability and age. Teams play to score against opposition

Progression(s)
• Limit touches on the ball
• Rotate all time attacker position

Key Factors
• Have as many numbers around the ball for options
• Every time a player passes the ball they must explode with speed in the direction they passed the ball

Communication Drill

Organization
As above, teams play 4 v 4 with one all-time attacker and goalkeepers in each goal. Players are not allowed to communicate at all, verbally or physically.

Progression(s)
• Make players communicate every time they make a pass or move to receive one and penalize by loss of possession of they don't communicate

Key Factors
• Get feedback from players on the three drills - when is communication most effective? How did they do with no communication?

ALSO AVAILABLE

VOLUME ONE

This book of coaching drills, exercises and small-sided games has been produced as a useful reference tool for you to browse through, as well as provide variations on ideas you might implement with your players.

Some of these drills you may have seen variations of and may have used before, others will be new to you. They have been collated from the author's (Rob Gale) playing and coaching experiences in the Score UK/ Fulham F.C. Academy, other drills have been adapted from many experienced and talented coaches who Gale has had the pleasure to work under or with over the years in various other English Youth Academies.

There is not an age or skill guideline on any of the drills. This is because sometimes a playful game can lighten the load of an experienced team and a tactical drill can be introduced to challenge a team of any level. It is our job as coaches to determine what drill suits our players at any given moment and which sessions will work to bring the best out of the players we work with.

Of course anyone can be a drill instructor, but your personality, enthusiasm and delivery of each drill to the players makes you unique as a "coach". Never be afraid to adapt or change ideas or sessions to your own style of practice. What works for one coach may not work for the rest of us. By imparting your knowledge of the game to the players – these become more than just drills

Why should your club have a Score UK Soccer/Fulham Academy?

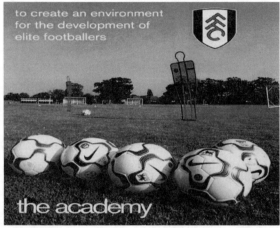

Because your players can go from playing here…

to having an opportunity of playing here!

UK SOCCER

PROFESSIONALISM

PROFESSIONALLY LICENSED STAFF – WITH PROFESSIONAL EXPERIENCE - PROFESSIONAL TRAINING METHODS
PLAYERS LEARN FROM A PROFESSIONAL CURRICULUM – FILLING OUT A PROFESSIONAL PLAYERS LOG BOOK –
PROFESSIONAL EQUIPMENT - PROFESSIONAL MEMBERSHIPS – ALL IN A PROFESSIONAL ENVIRONMENT

NEEED WE SAY MORE – THE ONLY PROFESSIONAL SOCCER ACADEMY IN THE WHOLE OF NORTH AMERICA – LINKED TO AN
E.P.L. CLUB… -Want to have an academy working with your club/association …

VISIT WWW.SCOREUKSOCCER.CO.UK FOR FULL DETAILS or contact 402 504 1718 / 402 883 5409

BEWARE OF WEAK IMITATIONS

BOOKS

$24.95

Item # 1011
This is the most comprehensive book ever written about the 4 - 4 - 2 formation. Covered are the roles and responsibilities of the defenders, midfielders and forwards in both attacking and defending situations.

BEST SELLER!

$29.95

Item # 1001
The most comprehensive book EVER published of soccer practices and training sessions. **Over 200 pages** full of training sessions from **Manchester United, Brazil National Team, PSV Eindhoven, Boca Juniors,** etc.

1,000's ALREADY SOLD!

$29.95

Item # 1014
Over 100 training sessions from the world's top teams like **Manchester United, Ajax, Liverpool, Juventus, PSV Eindhoven and São Paulo**. These, plus sessions from National teams from **Holland, Italy, USA** and others make this book a "must have" for any serious soccer coach.

$19.95

Item # 1007
This one-of-a-kind book shows every training session, practice and drill of the Penn State soccer team from their 2001 season where they reached the NCAA Tournament round of 16.

$24.95

Item # 1013
This incredible book shows every GOALKEEPER training session, practice and drill done by the New England Revolution from their 2002 season.

$19.95

Item # 1009
A great NEW book by **Anson Dorrance**. *Vision of a Champion* is a unique blend of technical advice and powerful inspiration that gives youth players, parents and coaches the secrets of over 25 years of success developed as a collegiate (University of North Carolina) and U.S. National Team coach.

$12.95 $12.95 $12.95 $12.95

All Four Books

$39.95

Item # 1002, 1003, 1004, 1005 - All four books # 1006
These excellent books contain material from the 2000 and 2001 issues of the WORLD CLASS COACHING magazine. Each book includes training sessions from the world's top teams like **Manchester United, Liverpool F.C., Juventus F.C., Ajax F.C., PSV Eindhoven, São Paulo** plus many of the **MLS teams**. Each training session includes a detailed explanation and is accompanied with easy-to-read diagrams.

$14.95

Item # 1010
This book is perfect for both the knowledgeable and inexperienced/ parent coaches of 9 - 12 year old teams.

Included are 32 complete training sessions covering **passing, receiving, dribbling, running with the ball, shooting, defending and goalkeeping**. There are also 16 fun, small-sided games that can be used in any training session or as warm-ups.

$14.95

Item # 1008
This book is perfect for both the knowledgeable and inexperienced/ parent coaches of young teams.

Included are 32 complete training sessions covering **passing, receiving, dribbling, running with the ball, shooting, defending and goalkeeping**. There are also 22 fun, small-sided games that can be used in any training session or as warm-ups.

To Order Call
1-888-342-6224

OR VISIT

WORLDCLASSCOACHING.COM

BOOKS & VIDEOS

Item # 1008

This book is perfect for both the knowledgeable and inexperienced/parent coaches of young teams.

Included are 32 complete training sessions covering **passing; receiving; dribbling; running with the ball; shooting; defending and goalkeeping**. There are also 22 fun small-sided games that can be used in any training session or as warm-ups.

$14.95

Item # 1010

This book is perfect for both the knowledgeable and inexperienced/parent coaches of 9 - 12 year old teams.

Included are 32 complete training sessions covering **passing; receiving; dribbling; running with the ball; shooting; defending and goalkeeping**. There are also 16 fun small-sided games that can be used in any training session or as warm-ups.

$14.95

Item # 1001

The most comprehensive book EVER published of soccer practices, drills and training sessions. **Every page** is full of detailed observations of the training sessions of teams like **Manchester United, Brazil National Team, PSV Eindhoven, Boca Juniors,** and many of the **MLS teams**. All include easy-to-read diagrams of each practice.

THOUSANDS ALREADY SOLD!

$29.95

Item # 1009

A great NEW book by **Anson Dorrance**. *Vision of a Champion* is a unique blend of technical advice and powerful inspiration that gives youth players, parents and coaches the secrets of over 25 years of success, developed as a collegiate (University of North Carolina) and U.S. National Team coach.

$19.95

$12.95 **$12.95** **$12.95** **$12.95**

$39.95

All Four Books

Item # 1002, 1003, 1004, 1005 - All four books # 1006

These excellent books contain material from the 2000 and 2001 year issues of the WORLD CLASS COACHING magazine. Each book includes training sessions from the world's top teams like **Manchester United, Liverpool F.C., Juventus F.C., Ajax F.C., PSV Eindhoven, São Paulo** plus many of the **MLS teams**. Each training session includes a detailed explanation and is accompanied with easy-to-read diagrams.

Three-Tape International Coaching Series
Featuring Coaches of
Manchester United - Liverpool F.C. - Leeds United

$34.95 **$34.95** **$34.95**

$89.95

All Three Tapes

Item # 2001, 2002, 2003 - All three tapes # 2004

In June, 2000 at Connecticut College, WORLD CLASS COACHING assembled on American soil for the first time ever, coaches from England's top Premier League teams, Manchester United and Liverpool F.C. for its International Coaching Seminar.

David Williams, Manchester United U19 Youth Team Coach and Sammy Lee, Liverpool F.C. Assistant Manager were joined by former Leeds United Coach, Mick Hennigan in this once-in-a-lifetime seminar. This three-tape series covers every session conducted by the three clinicians.

To Order Call
1-888-342-6224

OR VISIT

WORLDCLASSCOACHING.COM